"The questions are thought-provoking and the answers are intelligent and pointed always with a religious implication, and always with sympathetic insight and common sense." —*Fort Wayne News*

"In contrast to many advice columns which are made up largely of personal gripes or trivial matters with wise cracks for answers, most of the questions submitted to Dr. Graham seem to come from sincere people who are perplexed or troubled.

"In each case he appears to have thought through his answer as he tries to find a helpful solution. *My Answer* is a readable book in which many persons may find solutions to their own problems." —*Duluth News Tribune*

MY ANSWER
was originally published by
Doubleday & Company, Inc.

MY ANSWER

———◆———

Billy Graham

PUBLISHED BY POCKET BOOKS NEW YORK

MY ANSWER

Doubleday edition published November, 1960

A Pocket Book edition
1st printing .... August, 1967

The material appearing in this book is a collection drawn from Dr.
Graham's newspaper columns syndicated under the title "My Answer"
by the Chicago Tribune—New York News Syndicate Company, Inc.

This *Pocket Book* edition includes every word
contained in the original, higher-priced edition. It is printed
from brand-new plates made from completely reset, clear, easy-to-read
type. *Pocket Book* editions are published by Pocket Books, a division
of Simon & Schuster, Inc., 630 Fifth Avenue, New York, N.Y. 10020.
Trademarks registered in the United States and other countries.

CONTENTS

PREFACE

Everyone has a problem.

Wherever I go, I hear unhappy people asking for help. Perplexed and adrift, they cannot understand how they have lost their bearings. Instead of growing more serene with the passing years, they feel themselves pulled this way and that. With their families breaking up, their children running wild, and their own lives plunging toward the depths of personal degradation, they do not want to act as they do but they cannot help themselves.

Does the Bible hold an answer for them? Or for those persons whose difficulties are in the fields of business or ethics? Indeed it does!

For many years, I have searched the Scriptures for answers to problems that have come to me through my daily newspaper column, telecasts, broadcasts, and evangelistic crusades. I have written answers to these questions in a daily newspaper column called "My Answer," with a daily circulation of more than sixteen million.

There is overwhelming documented evidence that the answers based on the Bible have helped thousands. Young people have found guidance in difficult years of growing up—young married couples have been helped in the gravest period of adjustment—broken homes have been reunited and lives have been changed, as a Biblical answer has been given to the perplexing personal and social problems of our time. Business and laboring men have been prayerfully guided in the problem of ethics in critical and perplexing situations.

We have received several million letters in the last few

years asking every conceivable question, and presenting almost every possible human situation. Every one has received a personal answer either from me or from one of my able and faithful associates.

I have read many books and consulted many well-known professors of psychology, sociology, and philosophy—but always I have returned to the Bible for the basis of my answer. There is a burning conviction in my soul that our problems are a result of our ignorance of divine moral law, Judaeo-Christian ethics, and God's purpose for human redemption in Christ—our unwillingness to obey God's rule, suggestion and imperative for abundant living in any circumstances.

Now this book is called *My Answer;* my devout hope is that it might equally well be called God's answer. I have a far deeper conviction today than when I began that the Bible has the answer to every moral situation known to man.

From a mother whose heart is crushed because her son is in revolt to the husband whose wife is faithless, from the youth who wants one more fling to the aging saint who feels that he is not wanted by his children, the teachings of Jesus Christ provide the only ultimate answer.

It is my prayer that this selection of over three hundred questions and answers will be of help to you as you see your need expressed through someone else.

He who is "the Way, the Truth and the Life" can guide and help you to a new hope and courage to live joyously and abundantly in a difficult world.

BILLY GRAHAM

Montreux, Switzerland, 1960

MY ANSWER

Chapter 1

I Want to Get Married, But...

I am in love with a fine young man, but if I go ahead with our plans it will break the heart of my parents. To what extent is one obligated to parents?

The Bible teaches everywhere that we are to honor our parents, but it does not teach that they have the right to control their adult children. There was a period in life when you were directly responsible to them. You were to be obedient in all things. What they have forgotten is that such a relationship does not continue when adulthood is reached. You should still honor them as your parents, but you are not obligated to forego the joy of married life and your own family for them.

But there is another aspect to this problem. We sometimes discover the will of God through giving heed to the counsel of others if they are definitely committed Christians. I am sure you want God's will in the choice of a life partner. Consider carefully their point of view, but then make your decision, seeking the Lord's leading as you do so.

My mother is an invalid with no one to care for her but myself. Recently a fine young man has asked me to marry him, but he doesn't want to take the responsibility of my mother as well. I don't know what to do, and don't know anyone to go to for help but you. Can you make some suggestion?

It would seem to me that this young man who wants to marry you is not a sympathetic person or he would not so quickly refuse to accept any responsibility for your mother. Certainly this is a problem that most young people face in one way or another, but there is such a thing as Christian love and compassion which he seems to lack.

Your decision is not too difficult, for you would want and expect sympathy from your husband, but if he is not so by nature and by God's grace, he will probably be a cold and demanding person to live with. If you were the invalid, and your mother were well, what do you think would be her course of action? You can judge your own that same way.

I presume that you are at least nominally a Christian, though you didn't say so. As such, the Bible teaches that you should be in subjection to your husband (Ephesians 5:22). Should you marry this man, you should only do so if you are willing to live in that relationship, and accept his attitude in this matter as your own.

Certainly I would advise a heart-to-heart talk with your young man—showing him your responsibility and asking him to share it. Then commit the matter to God in prayer.

I am a woman twenty-one years old and in love with a man of thirty-five. He has been married twice and has five children by his first marriage. He says he loves me but won't divorce his wife. He claims that I am his only true love. I love him dearly, but I also have two children. Please help me. Should I forget him or make him take a choice?

My dear, deluded woman! Don't be the third sucker in a trio of suckers. This man is a typical philanderer, and will ruin every life he touches. Don't be deceived by these cooings of true love. That is a trick that has been used by every Don Juan since Adam.

You are young and your whole life is before you. God has given you two children. Better that you go through life without another romance than to make this beast the legal father of your children.

You've had your fling, I take it, although you didn't explain how you became widowed. You have at least had one more romance than most spinsters. Now settle down, grow up, and give the loving care to your children they deserve. Become a Christian, take an active part in the church, and God will compensate you for the tragedy in your life. Who knows, if you act like a lady, you might even find a respectable husband in God's time. But don't get panicky and fall for the first man who comes along.

The man who wants to marry me claims to be a Christian. So I could on that basis marry him. But every now and then he practices deceit, and it troubles me, for I cannot endure deception. Am I safe in marrying him, seeing that he is a Christian?

Just because a person makes the claim that he is a Christian does not necessarily mean that he is so. In fact, when you say this young man uses deception now and then, has it never occurred to you that he may be deceiving you when he makes the claim to a Christian faith?

Truthfulness and honesty are basic in the Christian way. Jesus said once: "I am the way, the truth and the life." In another place he said, "I came to bear witness to the truth." Truth is consistency. If this young man will deceive you in one matter, he may deceive you in many, for he cannot have respect for the truth.

David once confessed to God in his repentance: "Thou desirest truth in the inward parts" (Psalm 51, Verse 6). You can live with many other faults more easily than with dishonesty. By all means avoid it.

I am deeply in love with a young man who is about three years younger than I. He doesn't know my age and I am afraid to tell him. What is my responsibility?

There is no good reason why this should be a limitation on your marital happiness. In fact, statistics have shown that the average wife outlives her husband seven years. It is only a traditional thing that the wife is usually younger but it is known that some very happy marriages have the wife somewhat older than the husband. First, you should not deliberately deceive your friend lest you do much more serious damage to your love. You can gain his deeper love by complete confidence. Second, you should both recognize that love is something more than physical attraction. By making an issue of age, you admit that the physical is most important. There should be a spiritual unity developed in order to assure your happiness. This would depend on your common agreement in religious views. There should be a common field of interest, such as hobbies and recreation. There should be the possession of mutual friends and educational achievements. But more than all, there should be a oneness in Christ.

I am engaged to a fine young man. Since our engagement, I have come to realize that we are not spiritually agreed, and I am very uncertain about living with a person who has little faith in God. Am I doing wrong to break a promise I made in all sincerity if I break the engagement?

I would never advocate the breaking of promises. At the same time, if you go through with your proposed plans for marriage, you are going to make still more binding promises which you will not mean sincerely. If the young man is a man of integrity and decency, he will understand your change of view concerning marriage to him. When he understands that any marriage vow you would make would lack sincerity, and that you would make them only to fulfill your original promise to him, he should certainly release you from your troth.

Should the young man refuse to release you willingly, and he may not, then you must still insist upon your deep convictions as a Christian. In addition to this, your loyalty to Jesus Christ may be the very factor that will bring him to decide for Christ. Certainly your chances of winning him will be lessened after marriage. Make sure of full agreement on such vital matters before you make a life-commitment.

My fiancé and I have different religious views. We have talked it over and agreed that he is to follow his religion and I will follow mine. Don't you think we are on safe ground so long as we understand this? We deeply love each other and don't think religion should stand between us. We want your opinion.

My opinion would have to be based upon the plain teaching of the Bible. Your religion certainly shouldn't stand between you, but you do need a mutual faith to hold you together. Either you don't think religion is important or you have no definite convictions. Moreover, what would happen to your marriage if one of you should suddenly get some clear conviction. If you are so sure that your religion need not come between you, why did you inquire? You must have some doubts of your own, and rightfully so. I would urge you strongly to consider Christ and what He offers to hungry and lost hearts. Begin by taking Him as Saviour and Lord. Commit your lives to Him, and I am confident that then you will have a happy marriage that is built upon a firm foundation.

I have seen the difference in religion break up many homes. The Bible warns about "being unequally yoked." Be careful!

I am very fond of a certain young woman in the office where I work. We have had several dates, and I believe she cares for me. What I am not sure of is whether I really love her, and if there is any way that I can assure myself in this matter. Is there some help you can give me?

The popular conception of love as being just some kind of romantic feeling that should not be carefully investigated is very misleading. It would be well for every young person to move carefully in this area, for it is known that one out of four marriages ends in divorce. It is also known that divorced people have slight chances for solid happiness in any subsequent marriage. I would suggest that you first make sure that you share a mutual faith in Christ. Differences in religious beliefs are among the most persistent problems for couples after marriage, and especially when there are children. Second, I would recommend that you have as many things in common as possible. Your tastes, your friends, your hobbies, your educational experiences will all strengthen the bonds of marriage. Finally, I would urge you to consider the Biblical standard for marriage. If a marriage contains these elements of strength, it will produce more happiness as time goes on, even if the romantic elements are lacking at first. Feelings can deceive us in love even as they can in other areas of life.

I am a young man who is the product of a broken home. I am old enough that it should no longer trouble me, but my problem is that right now I am in love with a young woman who is also from a broken home. Do you think this would in any way influence our happiness in marriage?

All things being equal, it would seem to me that your chances for a happily married life would be very good. Having felt the pain of a broken home, you have probably learned the importance of laying a solid foundation for a home that will remain united and happy. The mistakes of your parents in both instances will serve as warnings for you that you do not fail in the same way.

In making your plans, I would urge you to be utterly frank and open with each other on all things so that no misunderstandings come. Do not base your love on a mutual sympathy because of your unfortunate experiences, but on genuine respect and admiration. Then you should include Christ in your planning. Even though many homes have some degree of marital happiness without Him, there is much that is lacking in any home when Christ is not received and honored. Have your time of worship together, confessing your faults and praying for each other. This will cement your lives to each other and the happiness you seek will be the result of God's blessing and presence.

I am in love with a very fine girl. Morally she is above reproach and socially she is always acceptable. But when I mention religion she flies into a rage. Don't you think this subject should be discussed by two people who are seriously in love?

I certainly do believe that one's relationship to God should be discussed, and that there should be substantial agreement on such matters before you take any final steps toward marriage. What a person believes is basic to his conduct and to agreement in many other matters. There must be something the girl is ashamed of or embarrassed about or she would not hesitate talking over the matter with you. This very attitude is already a barrier between you. Before you make final arrangements, be sure this barrier is gone. I receive hundreds of letters that indicate that unless two persons are agreed in their religious life they have slight chances for a completely happy life together. If the girl felt that there was agreement in the matter, she would talk openly about it. You have the right to insist upon an open and frank discussion to secure your future happiness and your usefulness under God.

The Bible warns about being "unequally yoked." I would advise breaking off this engagement unless this is settled by her coming to know Christ and entering into the Christian life.

My fiancée is of another faith. Now that we are making definite plans for the wedding we are for the first time meeting with innumerable objections. Should we proceed according to plan in spite of these objections?

You had better settle religious questions before the wedding even if it means a postponement. Your families no doubt waited until the last minute, thinking that you would not go ahead with your plans. You do see that there is a conflict and that there is no ground where you can stand in agreement. Some would advise that you simply agree to disagree, but that is not practical when two people will live as intimately as husband and wife. To have a happy life together, you must have confidence and respect, and you must have substantial agreement in your faith. The Christian loves Christ as well as believes in Him. It is much more than intellectual assent, it is commitment. Therefore, unless you reach a complete agreement, you will be happier to cancel your plans. "Can two walk together except they be agreed?" is always answered with a firm *no*.

A young man has asked me to marry him. Naturally, I'm quite flattered because he is a man of position, wealth, and physically attractive. However, I am certain that I'm not in love with him. Also, he doesn't seem to be interested in spiritual things. Should I marry him?

No. If marriage is begun with only a materialistic or only a romantic appreciation of its meaning, trouble lies ahead. A marriage founded on the basis you suggest loses its roots within a few weeks after marriage. A marriage founded only on a blind, optimistic affection is shattered as soon as the future brings disagreements and difficulties. There is certainly a definite place for physical desire and romantic affection, but if the relationship of the man and woman is intended to be permanent it must be built on more than either one or both of these. Genuine love is built on respect and spiritual affinity.

Certainly, you should never marry a man who is not interested in spiritual things. I take it from your letter that you are a Christian and that you go regularly to church. This very difference between the two of you will become a matter of severe disagreement in the days to come if you accept his invitation to marriage.

If you do not love him and he shows little spiritual interest, certainly you would be the most foolish of people to accept his proposition of marriage. Marriage is something holy, sacred, and spiritual. It should not be entered into lightly. If I were you I would rather die an old maid than to marry under such conditions as you describe. God also says: "Be not unequally yoked together." Certainly you would be entering an unequal yoke in violation of the word of God.

I am very interested in a young woman who comes from one of the society families in our city. She says she is in love with me, and I am with her, but we both are afraid of our social differences. Would you have any advice that would make our decision a wise one?

In America, there should be no such thing as social classes and class distinction. It would be very unwise to marry a woman who did not share your interests, who is either definitely inferior or superior to you in intellect and education. But the greatest blunder would be to marry one who does not understand your religious convictions and who is lacking in complete agreement with you. For lifelong fellowship, there must be many things you share in common. This makes for a rich relationship that is above the physical compatibility you may have. If these factors are present, the social differences are mainly superficial and should not constitute a barrier between you. Discuss these factors with her, and make certain that there is no area of your life or hers from which the other must be shut out. If you can work together, play together and worship together, you have then a workable combination. The question of the Bible is always "Can two walk together except they be agreed?"

I have been reared in a good home in a large city. The young man to whom I have become deeply attached is from a farm in western Kansas. While I think I love him, I do have an inward fear that I might not make a farmer's wife, because I have so little preparation for that calling, and I might not like a farm on those broad and endless prairies.

You will do well to consider every angle of the proposition before coming to a final decision. While love is primarily a matter of the heart, one should also use his head when falling into love. Some young people never count the cost of leaving home, parents, and loved ones to live in some distant place, perhaps under difficult circumstances; with the result that quite quickly they develop a corrosive criticism toward their circumstances. This attitude can be destructive of true marital happiness. On the other hand, it is delightfully true that young hearts can be so wonderfully deep and true that they can be happy with each other and working for each other just anywhere in the world. If you really love this man out of the West, you can be the happiest bride in the world and become the best farmer's wife in western Kansas. Love will teach you your new and unaccustomed duties, and cause the absence of your family to create wider horizons for your outlook in helpfulness to him and to your new neighbors. Settle the matter with finality in your own heart to be completely his, and before long you will have settled down to a little grey home in the West. If you both have Christ, then your happiness is assured under any circumstances.

At fifteen I promised my parents to abstain from liquor. Recently I became engaged to a very interesting man, and he insists that I break my promise. He does not drink to excess himself and we have much in common, but I do not feel that I should break my promise. Should I give in to him?

By all means, no! To begin with, in these days of alcoholism, no respectable fellow should insist on a girl drinking. If he were all that he should be, he would be grateful that you have principles and convictions against alcohol. You say that he does not drink to excess. You should say "Not that you know of." Young women should be wary of a man who drinks, and insists that his sweetheart drink with him. Now, his insistence that you take up drinking may be a test. It is possible that deep down he doesn't want you to, but he wants to see if you can be influenced. No person is less a person because he is an abstainer, but many people degrade themselves by imbibing. To me, the lowest of characters is the person who wants to pull everyone down to his level.

Have you prayed about this relationship? If I were you, I would seek God's guidance before I make the final plunge. Many homes in America are being wrecked by drink, and if I were a clean, Christian young woman, I would think twice before I married a fellow who is an "elbow-bender."

My wife-to-be is holding up our final date for marriage over the matter of what is to be done about children we might have. She wants me to sign papers, giving her right to raise them in her church. Are such papers legal?

Yes, such contracts are legally binding, and have been upheld in courts from time to time. This fact is not usually faced in time, and the custody of the children could even be given to someone else in the event of her death unless you fulfilled the terms of the contract.

The young lady evidently has strong convictions. Do you not have a positive faith? So often it is true that those with an indifferent attitude toward the Church are drawn into such an agreement that could well create problems in some distant future. You had better face the bold facts that a marriage that is not begun in harmony and agreement over such matters has little hope of long-lasting happiness. Successful marriage must be based on something more than a romantic feeling.

Chapter 2

When Trouble Enters Your Home

After two months of married life my wife and I seem farther apart than ever. In fact, we both wish we had not married. Can you tell what has happened to our love, for we did love each other?

If your love was real there is every reason that you should continue to be in love. Right now you are experiencing a period of adjustment that is always a testing time. Problems are new for both of you, and you probably both wish to have your pattern of life remain intact. This you cannot do. You must face the fact that you will both have to yield in many things and change some or many of your established habits and ways. Time will solve much of this problem.

There is an immediate step you can take, and it is one that has met the need of countless young couples. There are basic spiritual problems and conflicts. When two people are unable to make adjustments, there is a third party who will become a part of your home and your union and He can solve this problem. Jesus Christ can transform your personal life and can transform your home. He can do it by causing you both to end living for self and to begin living for Him. He will make a new relationship for you.

My husband and I have been married a little more than a year. Until I became a Christian we got along very well, but since

*received Christ we seem to argue all the time. I am at the
point of leaving him but want your counsel.*

The Apostle Peter had something to say about this. He said:
"Ye wives, be in subjection to your own husbands; that even
if any obey not the word, they may without the word be
gained by the behavior of their wives" (I Peter 3:1).

This is no easy assignment, but the responsibility is upon
you, not on your husband, to live a life that will challenge
him to make his own decision. This cannot be done by nagging and lecturing, but by the manifestation of a spirit of
meekness and submission that he has not discovered in you
before. Whether it is the husband or the wife who is the
Christian, as a Christian he must always accept and expect
some ridicule and even mistreatment for the faith. Just bear
this in mind: no one is in a better relationship to win the
other to Christ than a life partner. If you fail, probably no
one else will succeed.

*My wife and I have been married for four years. A short
time after we were married, all the romance went out of our
lives. How can we regain the love we once had?*

A romance enjoys the stimulation of high human emotions.
Most of them run, quite naturally, under their own power.
But a successful marriage is something two people must
work at if they want the spark of love to continue. The wife
you see when you come home in the evening with her "dish-
water" hands is quite a different person from the girl you
once courted with stars in her eyes. And, I dare say that
when you come home from your work, that you bear little
resemblance to the Don Juan you used to be before you were
married. You now see each other, not in an artificial aura,
but beneath the glare of reality. But marriages need not bog
down if both husband and wife make the least effort to be
a good mate. The woman who has taken you with all your
faults, for better or for worse, in sickness and in health,
should have your utmost respect and love—and vice versa.
Courtship is the vestibule to marriage. As mature, married
people, you cannot go back to your courting days. But your

love can deepen as the years go by. You have entered a deeper, closer relationship than courtship. Don't long for the porch when you live in the house. If you would put half the effort into marriage that you put into your courtship you'd be surprised how things will brighten up.

My husband and I were forced to marry when we were children. We are not really happy because we both wonder if it would not have been better to make our own choice. Would we be doing wrong to separate?

It seems to me that the only thing bothering you is that you didn't make the choice yourself. Your letter doesn't lead me to believe that you really do not care for each other. Now that you have lived together for a time and have made other adjustments, it would be your best assurance of happiness if you simply accept the fact that you are man and wife, and not think in terms of what might have been your own choice. I cannot approve the plan of someone making the choice and forcing you to accept it, but now that it is an accomplished fact, why don't you do what is necessary for satisfactory married life? In America today we place too much stress on the romantic aspect of marriage and too little on the practical. If you can respect each other, and if you are people who have some common interests, then if you would lay a spiritual and Christian foundation, you could have a more than average happy life together in spite of the unusual way in which you became man and wife. Let Christ be in first place for both of you.

I have absolute proof that my husband is being unfaithful to me. We have been married ten years and have three children. What shall I do?

There are three things you must consider and in all three you must ask God's guidance and help. First, your husband's soul is at stake and he needs to recognize his sin and ask

God's forgiveness. Ask God to give you the grace and wisdom to face your husband with this sin and let him see that you love him and are concerned over his soul's welfare. It may be that God will use you to resolve this problem and win your husband at the same time.

Second, yourself: your heart is heavy and your pride is hurt and this is a great burden which you have. Again you must pray for the love and grace to do the right thing. You can leave your husband but the problem is still not solved. If he can be won back, it will be far better.

Third, you must consider your children. If you separate from your husband your children immediately face the problems of a broken home. This can have serious consequences for them. They need a father, just as you need a husband. Also, despite what he has done, he needs his wife and children. Let me urge you to pray earnestly about this and then act in the wisdom and strength God will give you.

I have a fine husband but I have been unfaithful to him. Now I realize how very wrong I have been. What should I do?

In the Bible we are told that when David realized that he was guilty of a similar sin he cried out to God for forgiveness and that he was forgiven. Read the 51st Psalm after reading II Samuel, chapters 11 and 12. Here you will see the conviction of sin, sorrow for sin and turning to God for forgiveness are the steps to cleansing and pardon. David's sin had been known to many and the prophet Nathan told him he had caused "the enemies of the Lord to blaspheme." In your case public confession of your sin could do more harm than good. You should refuse to associate again with the other guilty parties. Having confessed your sin to God and asked Christ for forgiveness, ask Him also for the strength to live a life for His glory. Show your husband how dearly you love him. Try to be the best wife, homemaker, mother, neighbor, and friend possible. Remember you can never do this in your own strength. Ask God daily for the necessary power to overcome sin and live for Him. Spend time in Bible study and prayer. If you do these things you will find the sordid past will become only an unhappy memory because Christ has become both your Saviour from sin and the Lord of your life.

My husband is in many respects a good man and a fine Christian, but he does not like to work and is constantly absent from his job. I'm afraid he will soon lose it. He says that he doesn't worry because God will provide. Do you think God will provide in such a case?

From the beginning God so ordered the world that there would be adequate supply for man's need. Through sin, God ordained that this yield of the earth would come only through the sweat of man's brow. Work is a part of our lot in life, and to seek to avoid it is to seek to revoke one of God's basic laws of life. There may be some physical reason why your husband lacks energy, and this should be checked through your family physician. There may be a psychological reason why he avoids it, and in such a case, a competent counselor might help him. When he says that God will provide, he is telling that he is most impractical in his view of God and the promises of God. Work is co-operation with God in securing the supply. God will work with those who adjust to His laws and ways. Man's life is most happy in co-operation with God in every way. Point out to your husband the way of working with God and in making provision for daily needs through work.

My wife and I have been having bitter quarrels as to whether to have another child right away or not. We have three wonderful children and I want another immediately. My wife would like to postpone it.

Surely a woman is entitled to choose when she will undertake the burden she alone must carry in bearing a child. Motherhood is a beautiful, spiritually exalting experience, despite its hardships, if it gives expression to the heart's longing for a child. But when it is unwelcome and accompanied by consequent bitter thoughts and emotions it is merely a tragic, unlovely, physical ordeal. No woman should be called upon to pass through it involuntarily nor should she be obliged to live in constant dread of doing so.

In my opinion you are totally in the wrong. You and your wife should lovingly and prayerfully agree on this point.

The very fact that you are having quarrels indicates that your home is not a victorious, Christian home. I would suggest that you start Bible reading and prayer immediately; that you go to your wife and confess that you were wrong, asking her forgiveness. I am sure you will get it. Any home that is based on anything else than spiritual affinity is in danger.

Many nights each week my husband doesn't come home until nearly twelve o'clock. I still love him and don't want a divorce. What should I do?

Tell your husband you love him, and try to show it in little ways. Don't greet him with nagging and complaints. When you expect him home see that the house is in order, and be as careful of your personal appearance as you were in the days when he was courting you.

Don't imagine your husband is doing wrong if there is no just cause, but ask him directly what is keeping him out late. If it is pleasure, arrange more often to go out with him. Perhaps it will be necessary to make it plain to him that if your marriage is to continue he must be loyal to you, but first do all in your power to restore the love which once bound you together.

Have you both forgotten God? Marriages don't go on the rocks when a husband and wife take Christ into their home. Set aside a time each day to read the Bible and pray together. This has saved many marriages, and may help to save yours. If you both love God, and surrender your lives to Him, the gulf which now separates you will disappear.

My wife is expecting her first baby and her disposition has changed so I hardly know her. Sometimes I feel that she hates me and it is breaking my heart. What can I do?

I believe your physician can explain your problem to you and give you sound advice which will clear things up for both you and your wife. I am told that such changes occur at times like this and that they usually clear up spontaneously after the baby comes. Your wife needs your love more than ever and although it may be hard for her to reciprocate she will know that you are trying to be loving and considerate and it will help. I presume that you are a Christian, but in any case let me urge you to take Christ fully into your heart. Thank Him for this new life which is being entrusted to you two and pray daily that you may be given the wisdom and strength to raise this little one for Him. Let me also suggest that there is no married couple which has not encountered problems of adjustment and clashes in personality. These things can all be met and solved by exercising the mutual love and consideration which all Christians should have one for the other. Nothing helps more in a home than the family altar, a time when you and your wife join together in reading a portion from the Bible and praying together.

I recently married a widow who does not cease to talk about her first husband. I become very weary of this and wonder if I made a mistake in marrying her. Do you think there is anything unusual about this?

When a man marries a widow he should be ready to listen to a certain amount of talk about the first husband. He should be very realistic about the matter and not forget that the love of youth is much more romantic than the love of middle age. She probably married her first husband because of romantic love. She probably married you for more practical reasons. You do not need to feel that she is unhappy with her marriage to you, and you would be far better off to accept her reminiscing as the desire for something you are failing to give her. Perhaps what she wishes more than you know is for you to make some expression of love for her that you have not made. A box of candy or some flowers will do much to make her realize that it is better now than before. Neither can you afford to let your marriage continue without the benediction of God's presence in your lives.

I married a young man who had completely misrepresented himself to me. Right after we were married, I found he had been married and divorced, though he did not tell me, I had to find it out. I also find that he had been unfaithful to his former wife. Because of legal problems in his divorce I was able to have the marriage annulled. Now I am troubled over this, for I wonder if it is the same after all as a divorce.

There is a technical difference, for you did not have full information. I wonder that you would actually marry a young man with such limited knowledge of him. Did you not realize that marriage is a lifelong agreement? I rather believe that you base your marriage ideals on an emotional level, to the exclusion of the intellectual and reasonable. Whatever you may choose to do in the future, you must always be cautioned by this blunder. You must also recognize that the Lord was not leading you in this instance. Had you been in fellowship with Him, He would have led you along so that such tragedies would not come to pass. The reason I am not able to give you a clear answer is that I have no way of knowing the extent to which you consummated your marriage. This private knowledge would give you the answer, and you would then be able to make your next decision.

My husband became seriously involved with another woman. He has become a Christian and is thoroughly repentant but we decided to move to another town. Now this woman has followed us to this town. What shall we do?

Not knowing the status of the other woman, I can only advise you in a general way. I feel that you and your husband are to be congratulated on your mutual love and trust one for the other. You both have passed through deep waters and God has evidently given the forgiveness and grace needed. Let me urge you both to stick together as never before and to make all of your plans accordingly. I would completely ignore this other woman. If she makes advances, as well she may, be sure that she is given to understand that this affair is finished and that her presence is unwelcome. In all of this, let me urge you two to pray each day for guidance to meet the problems which may arise. Ask God to give you the wisdom and love and good common sense which will insure that this difficulty is met in His way. If the woman is a schemer, be particularly careful that she does not maneuver you or your husband into a compromising situation. I appreciate the difficulty and embarrassment of your situation but you have a source of help and blessing in the Lord Jesus Christ which will certainly see you through. Finally, pray for this woman: ask God to convince her of her sin, as he did your husband. She has an eternal soul for which Christ also died.

I am a Christian but my husband isn't. I think he makes unreasonable demands and is most of the time very disagreeable. How much must I take from him before I rebel and walk out on him?

No one can tell you the answer to such a question, without knowing exactly why you disagree so violently. It would seem to me that the Christian must always manifest the greater patience and understanding. Your willingness to submit to him at all cost, providing it does not violate your Christian devotion to your Lord, is that which will be most effective in winning him to your Lord. Insisting on your own rights will not always achieve the desired end. You don't really want to rebel and walk out. As a true Christian you want to influence him to recognize your Saviour and thus become a new person.

Only Christ can make a new person out of an old one. None of the ugly qualities of your husband are really the man you married, but they are that man under the domination of the forces of evil and of Satan. Pray that he will become a new person in Christ for the Bible says: "If any man is in Christ, he is a new creation" (II Corinthians 5:17).

I always thought that my wife was faithful to me. Last week she confessed to an affair with another man, and would not have done so except for the fact that she had experienced a religious conversion. Should I go along on a regular marriage basis?

Anything I would say might be interpreted as a liberal view on morals. Certainly the marriage vows should be adhered to and faithfulness is expected of both persons. But you must remember that if the religious conversion was genuine and one wrought of God, then everything has been changed. Your wife has become a new person in the eyes of God and you might well reckon her in that way yourself. She is not today what she was when she was unfaithful. This is the time to begin things over again. It is the time for new vows and a new family relationship can well be counted as beginning with her conversion. The Bible says: "If any man is in Christ, he is a new creature [creation]; old things have passed away; behold, all things have become new."

My husband is unfaithful to me, and I am told he is running around with teen-agers. We have a ten-year-old son. Shall I call it quits or what can I do? I am miserable.

You didn't tell me your husband's age, but such antics are not unusual for a man who is entering into waning manhood. His tendency is to blame his disinterest on the irresponsiveness of his mate, and in blindness to his condition, he seeks stimulation elsewhere.

However, I notice that you say "I am told he is running around with teen-agers." Women too pass through a stage when they become very suspicious of their husbands. Nature signals that the days of productiveness are coming to an end, and the first thought is: What will my husband do? Will he seek companionship elsewhere? Many marriages have broken up at this point, and in many instances the wife's false accusations were to blame. Before I did anything at all, I would make certain that my suspicions were justified. These are days when you need each other more than ever. It is tragic for people in middle years to dissolve their marriage. Above all, take Christ into your life. He will give you love and the desire to understand your husband. By all means don't call it quits, as you say. Make every effort to face this problem with faith in God, and in a mature way. The chances are that you can work it out and perhaps your happiest years together lie ahead.

I am married to a very wonderful person. In spite of the fact that I respect him very highly, I have fallen in love with another man who shows me the attention I crave, while my husband seems to take me for granted. I feel I can't break off with the one I love, but don't know how to bring the news to my husband. What is the right thing to do?

There should be no question concerning what is right. If you want God's answer, it would be that you forget the passing infatuation and settle down like any mature individual would. It is easy for another to show you attention when it only involves periodic favors and demonstrations without all of the responsibility of being married. If you still consider your husband a wonderful person and if you respect him, you are playing the part of a foolish child to entertain thoughts of infatuation which belong to high-school-age people. As far as taking you for granted, you should consider that a flattery, for it manifests the complete confidence he has in you. No doubt a woman likes to have much more romance than a man, but you have no assurance you would have more from your friend. Follow the Bible admonition and be obedient and submissive to your husband, and you will find him much more affectionate than you think. Secondly, this infatuation is a sin in God's sight. Confess it and allow this experience to bring you to a true relationship with Christ and your husband.

I was a divorced woman and several years ago I married a wonderful man whom I deeply love. Since then I have joined the church, and am living what I consider a Christian life. Now I am not sure if God will forgive me for my past sin if I continue to live with my husband. I have prayed for guidance but it seems that I receive no guidance from God. Please won't you tell me what to do?

You are one of the thousands caught in the modern vortex of divorce. But two wrongs do not make a right, and it is difficult to unscramble eggs, as we say. You say you are worried that God will not forgive you. Such worry is unfounded for the Bible says that He will forgive every sin that we truly repent of. Another separation would only make matters more complicated.

Since your past life is the chief matter of your concern, I would try to make up for lost time and lost opportunities by trying to improve the future. The Bible says: "Forgetting those things which are behind and reaching forth to those things which are before, I press toward the mark of the prize of the high calling of God in Christ Jesus." Satan would divert your gaze to the dark past, but God would have you look to a bright future of service and usefulness. Let the faithfulness of the future match the unfaithfulness of the past.

How many times should I accept my husband coming back to me? He has already left me three times and now wants to come back home again.

A good wife will do whatever she can to maintain the ties and bonds of the home. However, unless there is a real change of heart on your part and on the part of your husband, this same old process will go on indefinitely. What you need is something that will bind the home together. There is nothing that compares with a mutual faith in Christ to unite husbands and wives and to provide a proper foundation for a happy and satisfying home relationship. Christ teaches we are to forgive seventy times seven. With forgiveness, tenderness, understanding, love and prayer you should try to win your husband to Christ. He will never be different till he has a new nature.

Is it necessary to confess all of the details of a sinful life to one's mate after marriage? If so, should this confession include the names of anyone in sex sins?

It is unfortunate in a marriage if there is an array of sordid memories of past sins on the part of either partner. If young people could only realize that a happy marriage depends not only on the present, but upon the past, they would be more reluctant to enter into loose, intimate relations with any-one and everyone. Many a marriage has been imperiled by the backlash of past sins, which were not just confessed, but "found out."

As to the necessity of confessing past sins to one's mate, I don't think this is always advisable or necessary. I have known of homes that were wrecked by such confessions. The main thing is to confess any past wrongs to God, resolve to be true to your marriage vows, and absolve the black past by a spotless present. The Bible says: "If we confess our sins unto Him, He is faithful and just to forgive us our sins, and to cleanse us from all unrighteousness."

When I was very young I married, but our marriage ended after less than two years. With my second husband I have had two lovely children, but I am troubled all the time about something I heard concerning divorce and remarriage. Am I living in sin because I had a husband and separated from him?

Until we come to Christ, all of our lives are sinful and wrong. That is why God has provided a salvation that covers and removes all of our sins and makes a new creature out of a sinful and sinning one. Because you have trusted Christ, He has forgiven all of your past sins. The Bible always speaks of the sin of the people of God, putting away a husband or wife for the express purpose of taking another (Matthew 19:1–10).

My counsel to you is that simply thank God that He has actually forgiven your past, and then propose to live entirely for Him. Be the kind of devoted wife and mother you should be in the light of your present Christian faith. If God has forgiven your sins, why should you continue to re-fuse to forgive yourself? You are not glorifying God as you should unless you take His forgiveness and the freedom He secures for us (Galatians 5:1).

I've been married for eleven years to a man twenty-four years older than I. For five years he has been sick with a heart condition. He is good to my child and me, and is a good provider. I believe my health would be better if I left him, as he complains every day. What must I do?

You have evidently forgotten the vow you took at the sacred altar: "I will love, honor, and obey, in sickness and in health, until death do us part." You should have considered the difference in your age, and reckoned that your husband would age faster than you before you entered into the marriage contract. You say he is good to your child and you and is a good provider. It seems the only thing he has done wrong is to get ill, and he certainly has no control over that.

I suggest you repent of your selfishness, and ask this good man to forgive you for ever entertaining the thought of leaving him. With an attitude like yours, I doubt if a younger man would put up with you. Pardon me for being so frank, but I would like to shock you into thinking straight about this problem. Thank God for a good, though aging husband, and provide some happiness for him in his trial of affliction.

How can people untangle their lives? I have been divorced and am married for the third time. My wife has been married twice. Both of us know that we have been sinners and about a year ago we both were genuinely converted. But we see no way to clear up the mess we have made of our lives, and of the lives of others in the past.

You both have given your hearts and lives to Christ and you will just have to leave the entire matter in His hands of love. It is a moral, physical and legal impossibility for you to recover the lost years or to change those things which are past. When you accepted Christ as your Saviour you asked Him to take you just as you were. You have sinned but true repentance has brought true forgiveness. Our Lord said that He had come to save sinners, not the righteous. Therefore, you have the right to trust in His love and His redeeming work in your hearts. There are sins for which restitution can be made. In your case restitution must show itself in lives lived for God's glory and in helping others to find and know the same Saviour Who has saved you. Do not spend your time living in the past—look forward to a future spent in close fellowship with Christ. There is no sin too great for Him to forgive, so thank Him for His grace and mercy and praise Him every day.

I would like to clear my conscience. You see, I was married, then I deserted my first wife with two children, and now I am married illegally to a younger woman with no children. I have not divorced my first wife. What would be the Christian thing to do at this time?

You understand that it is difficult to give a clear answer, for there must be other details in your tangled affair that you have not disclosed. It is clear that you have wronged both women, and in addition have offended God through your past conduct. On the surface it seems that you are clearly the husband of your deserted wife, and that your present situation is not a marriage either in God's sight or the state's. You are also responsible to your children. The wrong you have done can never be undone and you must bear the scars of it throughout life. The better thing would be to resume your first responsibility; that is, if your former wife will have you. Then you are obliged to do all in your power to amend the wrong done to the woman with whom you now live. Finally, you must rely on the pure mercy of God for His forgiveness. Christ died for all who have sinned and come short of God's glory. Your only hope for eternity is with Him. Confess Him as Saviour, and turn from your sinful way of life to serve Him.

My husband has become seriously involved with other women, yet he thinks that I do not know about it. His friends say that he feels that he is doing no wrong in carry-

ing on what he terms a clandestine friendship. Do you think I should tell him that I can no longer stand his unfaithfulness after almost nine years of married life?

I must frankly say that your meek silence is in part to blame for your husband's philandering. He either thinks you don't love him, you don't care, or that you are not smart enough to know what is going on right under your nose.

By all means make him face up to this matter, and do it immediately. It may shock some sense into his head and awaken him. He's had it pretty good up to now, he thinks. Why shouldn't he continue affairs, if there is no conscience on his part, and no complaints upon yours? It evidently hasn't occurred to him that he is breaking God's law by committing this sin.

It is surprising what a show of spunk on the part of a wife can do in mending the ways of an erring husband. I've known men to grow up over night when wives reminded them that from now on it is an "either, or" deal. When either mate flouts God's law of faithfulness in marriage, someone must pay, and it might as well be the guilty one.

I am greatly concerned about a matter of importance. I was married and two children were born. My husband became involved with another woman and we were divorced. Shortly afterward I married a good man who has been a faithful father to my children. After studying the Bible and praying for God's will in our lives, I have become puzzled as to whether I was right about my remarriage, even though I was the innocent party in the divorce. Have I sinned and caused my husband to sin?

According to Jesus' words, divorce is never permitted except for unfaithfulness. He said: "Whosoever shall put away his wife, saving for the cause of fornication, causeth her to commit adultery: and whosoever shall remarry her that is divorced committeth adultery" (Matthew 5:32).

Some interpret this to mean that in case of unfaithfulness, the innocent party is justified in remarrying. Others say that the divorce is justified but that remarrying is not allowed. It all boils down to a matter of conscience. You say you are praying about the matter. I am sure you will be given guidance and direction.

Some things are difficult to undo. Eggs cannot be unscrambled—scars cannot be removed. You are remarried and another divorce would only make matters more complicated. My prayer is that God will make known His will to you and give you peace. Christ can forgive all past sins and mistakes. Come to the Cross and let Him touch your life.

My husband is away on business most of the time. Do you think it advisable for me to plan some life of my own and not depend on him for all of my happiness? Would it be wrong to have men friends?

When you made the marriage vows, you promised to remain faithful through all experiences. "For better or for worse" is the usual promise. Now you seem to regret having made the promise. But it is thrilling and wonderful to discover how the Christian view of life answers the most difficult questions.

For the Christian, marriage is a union in which three, not just two, people are involved. Those three are the husband, the wife, and Jesus Christ. Both the husband and the wife are completely committed to Jesus Christ first, and then to each other. Both seek to do His will, and not their own. By such an arrangement, happiness in the home is secure. Unhappily, you have depended on your husband alone for your happiness, and now you feel you must include a substitute in his absence. But this will only lead to grief. I urge you to consider Christ, taking Him into your life and into your plans. The Bible says: "Delight thyself also in Him, and He shall give thee the desires of thy heart."

On account of my husband's business, I am left alone much of the time. A woman becomes weary with other women at times, and I wonder if any harm would be done by having occasional friendship with a man friend who frequently invites me to dine with him?

If past experience can teach us anything, it is that such platonic friendships frequently lead to serious trouble and the broken home results. If you knew what your husband's business demands were before marriage, you had better live up to your vows made at that time. Have you talked it over with your husband, telling him of your need of his being home more than he is, or are you just playing the part of the spoiled child who wants everything for his own benefit? It probably isn't enjoyable for your husband either.

I would suggest three things. Try to have a frank talk with him at the next opportunity. Perhaps some solution can be reached. Make it a spiritual matter, in which you take your problem together to the Lord in prayer. Someone has rightly said, "More things are wrought by prayer than this world dreams of." Finally, you had better face the blunt fact that your desire for male friendship in your husband's absence is bound to lead to intimacy that you now cannot foresee, but which happens in most such cases.

Is a clandestine friendship an innocent thing for a married man to indulge in if he is not actually unfaithful to his wife?

I can but wonder why you ask this question, for an uneasy conscience has prompted it in the first place. How can a "clandestine" friendship, such as you mention, be an "innocent thing"? Unfaithfulness to your wife goes much deeper than a physical relationship with someone else. Participating in a secret friendship with another woman involves several moral issues which need to be frankly faced. You are wronging your wife, for she had the right to expect of you the unshared devotion and personal loyalty which evaporate when you begin seeking the close friendships of others. You are also wronging this other woman, for you have no moral right to give her the attentions such a friendship naturally involves. You are wronging yourself because you are fostering a divided relationship, which can, and so often does, lead to marital infidelity. Finally, you are sinning against God for He has told us that the husband-wife relationship is one of earth's sweetest and must be cherished with every power at our command. Instead of doing this, you are living a

double existence and you are playing with fire. What can
so easily start as an "innocent friendship" has within it the
seeds of untold sorrow for all concerned and of the eternal
loss of your soul.

*Six months ago my widowed mother came to live with us.
She is smart, capable, and loves us all but has proceeded to
take over our home and is trying to completely dominate me,
my husband, and our three children. We all are Christians
and I want to do the right thing.*

The right thing for you to do is to have a frank and honest
showdown with your mother. Do this only after you have
asked God to give you wisdom as you talk. Then, be sure
that you show her the love and appreciation that she deserves. At the same time, make it clear that it is necessary
for you and your husband to run your home according to
the best wisdom and experience that you have. I have the
feeling that your mother will recognize the mistake that she is
making and change her attitude. If she does not, then I would
prayerfully consider making arrangements for her to live
nearby where you can exchange visits but where at the same
time you will have the freedom to run your own home. Before you do any of this it may be most wise for you to re-
evaluate your own conduct and the way you conduct the
affairs in your house. It is just possible that some of the
changes your mother has tried to institute are wise ones. In
all of this, take your husband into your fullest confidence and
take no step without first asking God's blessing and help.

*My husband is permanently invalid. We are both rather
young, and I feel I am missing much of life. Would it be
right for me to commit him to a home?*

When you were married, you promised to cleave to each
other until death do you part. You will have to answer your
own question on the basis of your promise made at that time.
If a home or hospital is needed to give medical and thera-

peutic care, you would be right in sending him. If he needs the spiritual uplift that comes from the love of a faithful wife and the security of his own home, it would be both your joy and privilege to give him that care. Unless you are financially unable to maintain the home, it would appear that the right thing is to make a happy home for him. The Bible teaches that God made husband and wife to be one. Certainly in this time of his greatest need, you would not be the wife you should be to turn him over to impersonal hands to care for him so that you might have some freedom. This could be the most glorious and thrilling period of your life—serving a loved one. Certainly God would honor it.

Both my husband and I are very religious people. In spite of this, every two or three weeks my husband wants to go and see a burlesque show. He insists that he is doing nothing wrong—just looking. I think it is a sin to look at such things, don't you? It worries and upsets me.

The kind of conduct that your husband seems to enjoy indicates that though he may be religious, he is not closely following the teaching of the Word of God. Romans 13:14 clearly tells us that we are to put on the Lord Jesus Christ and make not provision for the flesh to fulfill the lusts thereof. Your husband cannot long stand the flames of passion without committing some sin sooner or later. It is an unnatural expression of the normal and wholesome sex life of any person, Christian or otherwise. Jesus said: "Everyone that looketh on a woman to lust after her, hath committed adultery with her already in his heart." This is the great danger, and no man can fix his gaze upon such expressions of sensuality and live an effective Christian life.

I was recently converted, and have been trying my best to get my wife converted. All I get is a sarcastic reply. She says it won't last, and that I had better live it before I start preaching to her. What should I do? I would like to have her experience what I did.

It is well that you desire so much the conversion of your wife. Every true believer seeks especially the salvation of his loved ones. Quite often, however, such things are the least understood in the home. Perhaps your wife is sincere when she says it may not last. I would offer these suggestions. First, give her a demonstration of what the Christian life is before you begin to persuade her too much. She will wonder what has taken place when she sees the change working out in everyday life. It won't be long until she will know that it is a lasting change, and then she will desire what you have found in Christ. Read I Peter 3:1. Second, show her that a Christian husband is far better than a non-Christian husband. All of the virtues of manhood are raised to the highest in the life of one who is surrendered to Christ. Finally, pray for her. More things are wrought through prayer than this world dreams of. God will answer your request in due time and you will have the joy of seeing her converted and your prayers answered.

My husband is not a Christian and will not go with me to church. He also insists that I engage in worldly things. I disapprove of these things, and he thinks that I am just being mean because he has refused to go with me to church. Am I wrong?

If you try to draft your husband into going to church, you are just as wrong as he is in trying to force you to do things which are against your convictions. Rather than being overinsistent that he go to church with you, it would be more advisable that you quietly and devoutly live the Christian life before him, and thus make it an attractive thing, rather than the boresome thing he evidently thinks it is. Many good wives are well intentioned, but get over anxious that their husbands immediately conform to their views. Often their insistence takes the form of "nagging," and no person is ever led to Christ in such a manner. I would suggest that you sweetly hold to your convictions and faithfully and patiently live the Christian life before him. No normal husband can long withstand the impact of a consistent Christian wife who prays for and longs for him to share her faith with her. Your disappointment may be part of the price you must pay for not marrying a Christian man in the first place. But "all things work together for good to them that love the Lord."

My husband, not being a Christian, resents my conducting family prayers and refuses to take part in them. Should I continue to have devotions with my children even though my companion will not take part?

My answer to your question is an unqualified "yes."

I strongly believe that if you are faithful in your witness for Christ in the home and continue having devotions with your family that your faithfulness will have a lasting influence on your husband and children.

But remember this: as spiritual leader in your house, your family will be watching your acts as well as listening to your words. I cannot conceive of your husband being able to long resist becoming a Christian if your conduct is thoroughly Christian.

Many well-meaning, devout mothers, in their anxiety to see their home united in the Christian faith, sometimes become almost demanding and often cantankerous in their zeal. A nagging wife will never win an unbelieving husband to Christ.

Yours is not an easy place to fill. The Bible teaches that the husband is to be spiritual leader of the home. So, you are forced to double duty because your husband is spiritually remiss. May God's Spirit guide you, may Divine wisdom be given you, and may heavenly patience be yours, until your family is completely united in the bond of Christian fellowship.

My teen-age daughter has an incurable disease. Should I continue to send her to school?

This is a question you must ask your physician. If she is still physically able to attend school, it would seem much wiser to let her attend school and lead as normal a life as possible and I believe that is what he would advise. As a Christian, let me advise you to make her life as bright and happy as possible, at all times letting her know that the hope of each of us is in Christ alone and that through faith in Him our sins are forgiven and we have eternal life. Try to make heaven seem a glorious place and something all of us should look forward to. Let her learn to read the Bible as a daily and happy experience of God talking to her. Make the fourteenth chapter of the Gospel of John and the last two chapters of the book of Revelation very real to her and try to speak naturally of all of those who know and love Christ going to be with Him someday. In this Christian instruction, be sure to make the home life as normal and happy as possible. Have her friends in for meals and to play games. Read interesting books aloud. Try to have as much laughter as possible in the home. God has given you a heavy burden but He will give you the grace and the wisdom to bear it for His glory if you will but trust Him for help.

Chapter 3

How to Help Your Children Grow

Sometimes our little boy refuses to say his prayers. What should we do then?

Don't try to force your child to pray. Every night set aside fifteen minutes or half an hour before his bedtime for reading and conversation. Show your child pictures of Jesus, and tell him stories of the Saviour. Talk to him of the Heavenly Father. Explain to him that God sends the sun and the rain. Tell him it is God who makes the flowers grow, and gives us food to eat.

Let your child hear you pray, using simple words he can understand. Say: "I like to thank God for the good things He's given me." Do this for a few days. Then some evening when you've finished praying, ask, "Isn't there something you would like to thank God for?" If your child says only a few words, be content.

There is no better way to encourage a boy or girl to pray. Later you'll want to teach your child to ask God to forgive the mistakes he's made, and to pray for strength to do what is right. But don't be impatient, or try to force your little one. Let him hear you pray. Surround him with love. Tell him of Jesus and the Heavenly Father. And soon he'll want to express his thoughts in prayer.

My wife and I do not agree on the matter of disciplining our children. I maintain that a child needs a firm hand, and a

spanking now and then. My wife says that all they need is
love and understanding. Who is right?

Both of you are partly right, and both partly wrong. They
need both discipline and love. Cold, harsh discipline without
love can do irreparable damage to a child. But an insipid
love that indulges the child and caters to his every whim
can also do great harm.

There is a great difference in children, too. I have one
child who rarely needs to be disciplined. Even if I spoke
to her reprovingly, her heart would be broken. I have another who responds to punitive discipline, and pays little attention to the "soft reproof." I think it is hard to lay down
any hard and fast rules because children vary so much. The
Bible teaches that discipline should be used when required.
But it suggests that discipline and love must go hand in
hand. It says: "For whom the Lord loveth He correcteth;
even as a father the son in whom he delighteth."

The lack of the right kind of discipline may indicate a
lack of love. It is much easier on the nerves to just let children go, than to plan and execute the kind of discipline they
need. But greater than discipline is the power of a good example. Children are more impressed by conduct they can
see than by lectures and spankings. If parents would live
the Christian life before them, it would have a tremendous
influence upon their children.

My wife and I have no church home. Now that we are par-
ents we would like to have our child christened but do not
know where to go. Can you give us some help?

You have a more serious problem than to find a place where
you can have your child christened. At the same time, it is
gratifying to know that you do have some spiritual concern,
for such concern is at least hopeful. The Bible says: "Train
up a child in the way he should go and when he is old he
will not depart from it." Your responsibility is to find the
full truth of the Gospel and to accept its provisions and
conditions for yourselves. Only when you have made a complete commitment of your lives to Christ and familiarized

yourselves with the message of the Bible can you do for your child what needs to be done. Find a church home where the Bible is preached and where Christ is exalted. Receive the Saviour for yourselves and then you will be in a position to provide the religious and spiritual home and background your child needs to grow spiritually as well as physically and intellectually.

My wife and I are wondering if it would not be better to keep our children away from Sunday school and church until they want to go? We do not wish to prejudice them in any way, but feel that they should make their own decisions.

I suppose you will keep them from public school also, lest their individuality be somehow distorted and their freedom restricted. Do you not realize that only those who are fully informed are really free to make wise decisions. The intention of a good Sunday school is to present to young people the basic truth of the Christian faith. A parent is responsible for the training of children and for affording them the best education available. Our whole concept of government rests upon the basic principle that people should be informed. We teach our youth the principles of democracy and the American Constitution so that they can vote intelligently. Why do you hesitate giving them a good basic teaching of the Christian faith, so that they can make a wise and enlightened choice? Someday God will hold you accountable for the religious training you either gave or denied your children. Give them the best you can, and above all, tell them the story of Christ and His love.

My husband and I have just become parents of a baby girl. Until now we have never thought of religion, and we would appreciate your help on how to begin.

The first realization of responsibility often makes us realize how much we need Divine assistance and guidance. Your coming to be parents makes you sense your responsibility to another soul. You must give her direction and instruction until she can make her own decisions. I would suggest that you first secure a Bible and begin systematic, thoughtful reading together. Begin with the Gospel of John. As you come to any particular Scripture that calls for any decision or action, accept it and act upon it. Questions of a critical nature can wait. As an example, when you read John 1:12, it says that "As many as received Him, to them gave He the right to become children of God." Ask yourselves: "Have we received Christ, and do we have the right to become children of God?" Continue that way of life through a personal faith. Above all, obey God's word and always settle each question as you come to it. Problems you can't understand will soon have their solution as you progress in your prayerful search for the truth.

In the school where my children attend, there has been much dishonesty and even some immorality. I don't like to have my children associate with such people, but cannot afford to send them to a private school. Are there any steps I can take to protect my children?

There is a danger of protecting our children too much. That is, we can withdraw them from society as it is until they come to have a pharisaic attitude. We must face the real situation. These dishonest and immoral children are a normal cross section of humanity and your children will always have to live in contact with them. The wise course of action is to give them the spiritual and moral training and example at home that will equip them for working and doing business with such people. They will be more likely to develop strong spiritual powers through opposition than through living in a situation where they never need to make decisions. The important thing is to give them the grounding they need in the Scriptures, let them see sin in its real light, and show them that with Christ as Saviour and as their guide, they can face opposition and win. Their small victories will prepare them for the larger battles ahead.

My husband and I adopted a child a few years ago. We decided never to tell him about it, but to let him feel that he was our own son. Now at the age of almost fourteen, he hears from another source that he is adopted. He has not mentioned this to either of us, but is very cool to us, even though we have sacrificed so much to make him happy. How can we make right this error in our dealings with him?

It will do little good now to say that such things had better be discussed openly. It would be much better if you had explained the matter to him long ago. It is no justification for his coolness, though, and I believe that he will understand a clear explanation. Any young man who has been given a fine home and cared for through his early years will know that what you have done has been done in love and generosity. There is only one thing you can do. Have a heart-to-heart talk with him, acknowledge your error, and tell him why you tried to make him feel that he was your own son. Assure him that your early love for him is just the same, and that all you desire from him is that he love you as foster parents and accept your care and kindness in the spirit in which you have given them through the years. It is the element of secrecy that is disturbing him now. Remove that and I am confident he will be very understanding. Make it clear that all that you have done has been in the name of Christ and for His honor.

I am writing for my husband and myself. We have a son who is unruly and undisciplined. We have tried to show him how much his disobedience hurts us and have tried to reason with him, but in vain. Although he is just a young teen-ager, we are afraid he is out of control. In our desperation, is there anything we have failed to do for him, or is there anything we can do to save him?

God may do for you what you have already failed to do for your boy. Discipline and the recognition of authority can seldom be taught when a child reaches his teens. Discipline and control begin at the cradle, just as your training in other matters begins there. It is no kindness to a child to permit him to have his own way in infancy and young childhood. He will pay for such liberties later and will cause you much sorrow.

Perhaps the problem now is a spiritual one. Perhaps the only place you can take the matter is to the Lord. God is patient and able when we call upon Him. I would say that you should first settle any spiritual problem you may have of your own. Take Christ as Saviour and Lord and give His word free course in your lives. Then ask God to somehow use your consecration to Him to influence your son for Christ. I am confident that although every other means may fail, if God touches the heart of your son, he will still grow to be a respected citizen and a loving and appreciative son.

Many modern child psychologists disapprove of spanking a child. What do you think?

I believe the real question lies in the effectiveness of the punishment rather than the method. Each child differs in temperament, and a patient, observant parent will watch carefully to note what is the most effective way to handle each child. Punishment is the negative part of discipline. While very necessary, we should also be careful to emphasize the positive angle. Keep children happily occupied. The Bible says: "A child kept to himself, bringeth his mother to shame." Keep children happily, wholesomely occupied and they will usually stay out of trouble.

We live in a crowded section of Brooklyn. My wife worries all the time for fear our two boys will join a gang. I'd like to move, but can't afford to. What do you think we should do?

If you and your wife are sincere Christians, and have led the boys to a personal faith in Jesus Christ, you don't need to worry about them. Ninety per cent of juvenile delinquency can be traced to careless homes. The Bible says: "Train up a child in the way he should go: and when he is old, he will not depart from it" (Proverbs 22:6).

I appreciate your wife's desire to move to a better neighborhood. Do that, if you can. But remember that some juvenile delinquents grew up in mansions, with servants to wait on them. It isn't a high ceiling, or beautiful furniture, or air conditioning that makes a fine home. What counts is the character of the parents, and the example they set their children. Let your discipline be governed by love. Be absolutely honest. The boys will know if you try to cheat the corner store, or the government.

See that the boys are kept busy, and given responsibility. This should begin when a child is three or four, and increase with each year of growth. Young people who gain satisfaction from their accomplishments seldom get into trouble.

As it has been said: Don't send your boys to Sunday school; take them. Go to church as a family, and bring your religion home with you. Invite Christ into your house. Speak and act as you would in His presence. Read the Bible and pray together every day. Establish a Christian home, and you can be sure your boys will seek good companions.

Our home isn't the same since we bought a TV set. The children leave the table before they've finished eating. My husband cares more about the programs than about me. What can I do?

You didn't say how long you've had your TV set. If only for a few weeks, I'm sure it will not always have the drawing power it does now. But in the meantime, good manners and consideration for others must not be forgotten. The Bible says: "Better is a dry morsel, and quietness therewith, than a house full of sacrifices with strife" (Proverbs 17:1).

If you once had a Christian home, where love and peace were found, surely your husband and children are missing it. Sit down as a family and discuss not only the use of TV, but rules you must follow to maintain an orderly, happy home. Let the children know what is expected of them. Don't indulge them today, and then scold tomorrow. However, sometimes it may be wise to change the dinner hour to let the children see a good program. Talk this over as a family. Decide, with God's help, what is best for all. Then stick to it.

This will be easier if you begin the day with God. Family devotions are as important as breakfast. Read the Bible and pray together. Ask God for guidance, and He will show you how to use all the good things He has given you. TV, like the family car, can be a disrupting force; or it can bring the members of your family closer together as you share the best it has to offer.

My ten-year-old son wants to spend all of his spare time playing ball. How can I keep him from wasting his time?

It is possible that he is not wasting his time as much as you think. Young people need the recreation and stimulation to be found in wholesome games. They have much excess energy and playing ball means much to young folks. This does not mean that he should be permitted to neglect home duties. These should be assigned to him and he should be required to carry them out. But, do not make his work a punishment: make it a share of the responsibilities all participate in. Then, let him understand that you want him to have a good time and I know of no better way than playing ball. It might be a good thing for you to go along some afternoon and watch the game. It means much to our children if they find we are interested in their sports and in their friends. Learn about the game so you can appreciate the plays. This will give him a feeling of your interest and that in turn will make him happy to tell you about his other experiences and friendships. Above all else let your boy know that you love him and are interested in what he is doing. His spiritual welfare must come first and if you prove to him your understanding in his boyish interests you have a stronger bond to help him in spiritual matters.

I hear you speak of family devotions. Is a family altar really practical in this streamlined age?

Family devotions are not only practical, they are *essential* in the well-adjusted home. I list below seven reasons why I consider family worship important:

1. It unifies the homelife, and puts faith in the place of friction.
2. It brings to the family group a sense of God's presence.
3. It shows the children that God is relevant to everyday living, and not just a Being to be worshiped on Sunday.
4. It gives members of the family an opportunity for self-examination and confession of sin.
5. It strengthens the members of the household for the tasks and responsibilities they are to face during the day.
6. It insulates us against the hurts and misunderstandings which come our way.
7. It supplements the work of the church, and makes of our homes a sanctuary where Christ is honored.
"And thou shalt teach them diligently unto thy children; and shalt talk of them when thou sittest in thine house . . ." (Deuteronomy 6:7).

Recently our young son has become very argumentative over everything that concerns our religious faith. We have always taught him the truth and until recently he accepted it. How have we failed that he should now question all he formerly believed?

All of the arguments your young son is putting forth against your religious faith do not mean that he has no longer any faith. He is right now at that age when he must base all of his convictions upon something other than what his parents believed. It is a most normal thing for teen-agers to question established beliefs. You will find that down in his heart, he really wants to have that faith confirmed, and he hopes you will do it for him. He wants to know why you have believed the Bible and how you first trusted Christ. You would have much more reason for concern if he became completely indifferent or passive. He wants to believe, but he must have a faith for himself, and not one that is just handed down. From you, he needs understanding and a good reason. The Bible says: "But sanctify in your hearts Christ Jesus as Lord, and be ready always to give an answer to every man who asketh you a reason for the hope that is within you yet with meekness and fear" (I Peter 3:15).

I am a Christian leader in my community. Recently I was embarrassed to find that my youngest son has been stealing. I have four other children, all of them examples of Christian training. Why doesn't this one follow in their steps? How can I save face in such a problem?

It is too bad you are only concerned about how the thing looks and how it reflects upon you. Your concern now should be for the boy. Most likely, the pride you have taken in your older children is one of the reasons why the youngest is now your problem.

God has given children to us as a trust, and often our usefulness is related to our concern for their spiritual welfare. The Bible says: "For I have known him to the end that he may command his children and his household after him, that they may keep the way of the Lord, to do righteousness and justice" (Genesis 18:19). There are two possible reasons for this deviation. Perhaps you have neglected this boy, seeing that the others have done so well, or you have made him resentful because of your frequent comparisons between him and the other children. Take time with the boy, and praying God's help, you may direct him into a right relationship with God and society as well. Let your concern be for his spiritual welfare rather than your professional standing.

My sister and her husband are wonderful Christians. They are kind and loving in the home, and yet one of their daughters completely rebels against the Bible, the church, etc. Explain this.

This is not at all unusual. In the Christian ethic, no one is forced to follow Christ. The Bible says: "Whoever will may come." Christianity is an involvement of the will, and no one can be coerced into becoming a Christian.

I have observed a number of rebellious children from Christian homes, but this is usually just a stage in the child's development. It is often a sign of strong character in the child. Some children take things for granted, and others will not accept Truth until they have examined it carefully. In the end, these types make the best Christians.

The Bible says: "Train up a child in the way he should go, and when he is old [mature] he will not depart from it." We don't want our children to be rubber stamps of what we believe, just to please us. We want their faith to be deeprooted and strong. Don't be discouraged if there is temporary revolt against Christ and His claims upon life. When they are mature, they will "not depart" from what is true and right. Some of the strongest Christians I know (including my wife) are people who were slow to accept the Truth of Christ in their late teens.

You keep insisting that we parents take our children to Sunday school. It seems to me that this is taking advantage of our authority and forcing them to accept a certain religious view. Don't you think it better to let them come to their own conclusions, and not force them?

According to the Bible, we all have a sinful nature (Psalm 51). If this nature is allowed to express itself, a person will invariably turn to sin and wickedness. By your failure to direct your children, you are not allowing them to make any choice but leaving them in spiritual ignorance. Certainly this is not the proper function of a parent.

As a parent you have the responsibility of directing your children in the ways of the Lord. The Bible says, "Train up a child in the way he should go, and when he is old, he will not depart from it." This also means that you must make sure that you know the way so that you can direct your children. Should you fail here, you will be like the blind leading the blind.

How responsible are parents for the conduct of their children? My husband and I are concerned as our son is rather a bad boy.

Apart from religious influence, the family is the most important unit of society. It would be well if every home were Christian, but we know that it is not so. The family and the home can never exert their proper influence while ignoring the Biblical standard. The Bible calls for discipline and a recognition of authority. If children do not learn this at home, they will go out into society without the proper attitude toward authority and law. There is always the exceptional child, but the average tells us that the child is largely what the home has made him. The prophet Eli was judged by the Lord because he had put his sons above Jehovah (I Samuel 2:29). The only way to provide the right home for your children is to put the Lord above them, and fully instruct them in the ways of the Lord. You are responsible before God for the home you provide for them.

My wife and I both work, she on a day shift and I at night. Our children are getting out of hand and we want to make a real home. How can we do it?

I do not believe you can have a normal home life under the conditions which you have described. First of all, a husband and wife need the companionship, one of the other. Working on different shifts as you are, this would be very difficult. Also, under this arrangement your children must have a sense of insecurity which could do them permanent harm. While jobs are important, your home is also vitally important and you alone are responsible for your children. You brought them into the world and it is your obligation to give them the best home possible. It is not things in the house which make it a home. Rather it is love and companionship and laughter and sympathy and interest in each other's lives and problems. Not knowing what kind of work you are doing, I can only suggest that your wife stay at home and make a real home and you take a job working in the daytime, so your evenings can be spent together. This will mean a smaller income but what profit is it to make more money, have your children unhappy and probably harmed, and even have your home go on the rocks? Most important of all, make your home a Christian home by asking Christ to live in your hearts and direct your lives. Have family worship by reading the Bible and praying together. If you do this, you may have less in this world but you will be laying the right foundation for eternity.

Chapter 4

What Every Teen-ager Should Know

Because I have grown up in a Christian home, I hate to as
my parents this question. Many things that have happene
in high school have made me wonder about God. How do
know there is a God? My parents would be hurt if I aske
them, but can you help me?

Until recently you have believed in God because your par
ents and your pastor believe in God. But don't be too dis
turbed about your doubts. There is a good reason for them
Every high school boy or girl goes through the stage of doubt
ing many things. I am sure you doubt other things you hav
formerly believed, but your lack of assurance about God dis
turbs you.

What you are doing is this, you are beginning to think fo
yourself. You no longer accept matters of truth on the basi
of your parents' say-so. You want reasons for everything
Faith has its reasons also. You can believe in God just lik
the scientist believes in relativity or atoms. He cannot se
either of them, but they are the only explanation for th
world as it is. Therefore he goes about his work, assumin
their truth and reality.

God is the only answer to the problem of existence, o
conscience and of many other things. The Bible says: "H
that cometh unto God must believe that He is, and that H
is the rewarder of them that seek after Him." On the basi
of faith, go to God and your search will be richly rewarded

48

My boy friend and I want to be engaged very soon but both of our parents object. Though we are quite young, we are serious but don't intend to get married for at least three years. Should we insist on doing it our way?

Perhaps your parents are objecting on the basis of your age alone. They perhaps think you aren't mature enough to make this all-important decision. There seems to be only one reason why you insist on an engagement, because you are afraid that one or the other might feel too free otherwise. I would warn you that if you cannot trust each other under the present conditions you are perhaps not genuinely in love. Then you must always take into account your mutual relationship to Christ. You must not hope for a completely successful marriage if it is done on your own. I would suggest, therefore, that you follow the suggestion of your parents. All they object to is the formality of engagement, and that is not the most important part of it. Your mutual commitment of your lives to Christ is all you need in addition to your love for each other to make your present friendship become even more meaningful in years to come.

Is it wrong to pet?

This question, because of its delicacy, has been evaded by some columnists. You have asked a sincere question, and I'm going to give you my sincere answer.

Petting, which is a popular name for promiscuous love-making between the sexes, can be very injurious to the person, to the conscience and to the personality, and therefore can be very wrong

Generally, it is a yielding to the lower impulses, and paves the way for looseness and even immorality. On the surface, it may often seem innocent and harmless. It has been argued that it is natural, and hence justified. But I am not alone in believing that it can bring great harm to the persons involved, if engaged in indiscriminately.

Let's face it, petting is the physical preliminary to more intimate relationships. Therefore, if the persons involved have no moral right to cohabit, they should forego the pre-

liminaries—petting. If engaged in promiscuously it can leav
the parties involved frustrated, conscience stricken, and ca
leave scars on the nervous system and personality.

Happy is the person who marries a mate who has not bee
pawed over. If intimate lovemaking was deferred until la
engagement or marriage, there would not be so many u
happy marriages. Don't play fast and loose with your em
tions and passions. Let them be under the control of Chris
and your life will be fuller and richer.

*How far should a young girl go in showing affection for
fellow in order to keep him from running to other girls?
like this fellow real well, but he makes unreasonable deman
in necking.*

You had better first decide why you show affection to th
young man or any other. If the only function of such a di
play of human affection is to keep him from running out wit
other girls, you had better let him go. Some physical contac
with a young man may seem to be a natural thing to do, bu
it is also a preliminary to the more serious sex acts of im
morality. That is why a young woman had better think twic
before she gives herself to any young man. Your aim is no
to achieve popularity by going as far as the young man de
sires, but to reserve your display of affection for the youn
man who will be your husband. Know the difference betwee
the showing of true affection and the giving vent to anima
passion, the difference between lust and love. Those who fa
to make this distinction are those who are soon in troubl
and who have a lifetime to regret their folly.

*I am a teen-ager and my parents treat me like a little chil
I have adult responsibilities, but kindergarten privileges. I ar
perfectly miserable. Can you help me?*

Growing up is hard, but remember that in any kind o
growth there are "growing pains." Keep in mind that this pe
riod in your development is also difficult for your parents. I

is not easy for them to realize that their child is becoming an adult, and they must make an adjustment as well as you.

It is my observation of some teen-agers that they want adult privileges but assume kindergarten responsibilities. Here is where the conflict comes between maturing children and their parents.

The main thing to watch out for is bitterness during this stage. Don't let the unpleasant events of these difficult years leave any scars that will hamper your future happiness, and make a breach between you and your parents. I strongly urge all teen-agers to accept Christ as their Lord and Saviour. Then when problems arise, we can say: "I can do all things through Christ which strengtheneth me." The happiest young people I know are those who have discovered the thrill of living for Him. When we are "reconciled to God," it usually follows that we are in harmony with others.

Almost all of my family and acquaintances are Christians. They keep telling me to read the Bible and find out how to live the Christian life. Honestly, I get bored when I sit down to read it and when I try to pray I keep thinking of a thousand other things. Is there something wrong with me?

I don't think there is anything wrong with you that is not typical of most young people. Having grown up in a religious atmosphere, you are right now passing through a period of revolt. You want to be on your own and make your own decisions without their influence.

There is another fact you should know. One of the devil's methods is to attack everyone, old and young, in this matter. He knows that the Word of God is powerful, and he will try to keep you from it. That means you are involved in a spiritual warfare.

If you would stop for a moment and think as a mature person, you would realize that your parents are trying to get you to do what is for your good. Don't rebel, but give God the opportunity to change your life and help you over the problems of youth, for they are many. Solomon once said: "Remember now thy creator in the days of thy youth," and this is what you should do to find the greatest joy.

As a group of young people, we are inclined to believe what you have been preaching. However, we want to have fun before we give our lives to the Lord. Don't you think it would be better for us to get this out of our system before we begin going to church?

Either you are making a very foolish decision or else you do not understand what the Christian faith is. The Bible says: "In thy presence is fullness of joy and on thy right hand are pleasures forever more." There is no life that presents a greater challenge or a greater thrill than living the Christian life. The Christian faith and life are as pertinent for the young person as they are for the old. Any person who has ever tried what you suggest has said what Solomon did (Ecclesiastes 12:1), "Remember now thy creator in the days of thy youth."

I strongly urge you to give your life to Christ now while the Holy Spirit is speaking to you. To postpone such a decision could prove disastrous. There is danger that while sowing your wild oats, you may also harden your heart.

Life in our small town is very dull. Any activity we try to get up is regarded as wild by the older people, and they say it isn't Christian. We kids get bored. Do you think that having a good time is wrong?

One of the reasons that young people are bored is that there is not enough activity to consume their energy. If you are a normal young person, you want to give yourself to something and spend your energy on it. Many old people forget that they once were young, and that is why they fail to understand your activity.

No one is bored who is creative. Only those who want to have everything done for them are bored. Therefore, plan some creative activity that will challenge the other young people. There are many wholesome games of competition that are enjoyable and clean.

No, having a good time is not wrong. It is when we abuse and misuse what God has given us that it becomes evil. The Bible says that "He giveth us richly all things to enjoy" (I Timothy 6:17). These gifts of God are for our use. To make sure what are the true gifts of God, apply the Scripture to all activity which says, "Whatsoever things are true, whatsoever things are honorable, whatsoever things are just, whatsoever things are pure, whatsoever things are lovely, whatsoever things are of good report," these are the things the Christian should accept and enjoy to the glory of God.

I am an eighteen-year-old girl, a freshman in college. I have fallen in love with a senior who wants me to marry him now although he has not yet made up his mind what his life's work shall be. Should I give up my own college career for him?

The very fact that you are weighing your own career against the uncertainties of marriage makes me feel that you are not yet ready to make this momentous decision. Obviously you have known this young man for only a few months. Also, his own future plans are so indefinite that they give you pause. This all adds up to a strong indication that you should wait. Waiting has two advantages. It will enable you to know your own heart and to decide whether it is love or other considerations which have attracted you two. Also, it will give both of you time to mature in your thinking and your planning. Finally, a Christian has the right and privilege of asking God's guidance in everything. Let me suggest that you put your trust in Christ as Saviour and Lord, then, as a child of God just ask Him to give you the leading of His Spirit. When you do this you may rest assured that the future is in His hands, not your own.

My mother and father are very ambitious for me to go to college, but really I am much more interested in learning a trade. I have a lot of tools and like to work in wood. Believe it or not, I would like to be a carpenter.

From your question I assume you are now in high school and facing the decision about your life work. At the moment you do not have all the facts you need to make an intelligent decision. You should respect your parents' wishes and seek to please them, yet at the same time, the life you will live will have to be your own. Your high school principal or counselor can recommend vocational aptitude tests for you, which, while not completely conclusive, can be very helpful to you in making a wise decision. If you are more adept at working with your hands than studying in the library, very possibly you should become a carpenter. No trade can be more honorable, and if I were you, I would prepare to be the best carpenter possible so that you may build for strength and for beauty. The job well done will be your deepest satisfaction. If you are a Christian make it a matter of definite prayer and God will direct you. If you are not a Christian, I would advise you committing your life to Christ at the earliest moment. Nothing can be sure in life until this matter is settled.

I am a student in a university, and was reared in a Christian home. I was shocked to find out that many students live for sex, and seem to have no moral restraints. I feel somewhat like a "fish out of water." Should I try to make an adjustment to this way of life?

Some young people still believe that they must "sow their wild oats." What they forget is that "Whatsoever a man soweth, that shall he also reap."

By all means, don't conform to those who have been overwhelmed by the tide of immorality which is sweeping our country! Professor Sorokin of Harvard says that America is a victim of a sex revolution that could ruin our nation. What will our future be if young people like you, with ideals and convictions, yield to the pressures to be immoral?

Many marital breakdowns can be traced to the loose morals of college years. "Wild oats" have a way of hounding people throughout the years, and springing up at the most embarrassing moments.

While there are some who laugh at a person with standards and ideals, most people will admire you. Our nation grew strong in an era when moral standards were emphasized, and it will grow weak when we condone that which we once condemned. Help stem the tide of adultery, divorce, and obscenity in America by standing true to your convictions. You are the kind of young person we most need in America.

I am a Christian student in a secular high school. In one of my classes, it is known that in order to get a good grade I will have to cheat on exams. Everyone else does it, and I wonder if it would be wrong for me to do so? I think that even the teacher knows that it is done but doesn't pay attention to it.

The conscientious Christian is always compelled to make decisions regarding morals and ethics. Often it seems almost right to be dishonest, especially when it is the general practice. It is in just such a situation, however, that the genuine virtue of the Christian is best seen. Our faith is never tested in an easy situation, but in the hard one. No matter what is at stake, you will still have your own conscience to reckon with, and you could never be at peace with God nor respect yourself if you in such a matter were dishonest.

You said that "everyone else does it." I think you are failing to recognize the many fine Christians who serve the Lord constantly in schools and shops all over the nation. Perhaps you have failed to contact them and observe their lives. Do not yield to the subtle temptations that present themselves, but live for Christ in every situation. After all, you must first please Him, and then other things will fall in line in due time.

Since coming to the university, I find that unless I join a sorority I am just left out of the social life here. Still I can't approve the program sponsored by those I know about. Is compromise the only answer in this world, or do I have to be on the outside?

Many times the Christian feels at odds with the world, and if we are to depend upon the words of the Saviour, it will continue to be that way. Jesus once said: "Behold, I send you forth as sheep among wolves." Although it may not appear that unconverted people are fitting that description, yet it certainly shows that there is no good way to effect a reconciliation unless they are reconciled to God first. In answer to your question about compromise, it will have to be said that when you do, only you are the loser. The very ones whose social pressure caused you to compromise will despise you for it. They respect your convictions and many of them wish they had the moral stamina to stand alone. May the Lord give you added courage to be a witness for Him, even in a hard place.

Don't be a prude, or be snobbish, but let your life "glow" for Christ. We are lamps shining in the darkness. Be attractive and winsome, but do not compromise your convictions for the sake of popularity.

How can I be a Christian and not be accused of being peculiar by the other kids in high school?

If you will keep the two things clearly separated you will find your problem so much easier. Being a Christian is the important thing and it involves a commitment of your life to Him as Saviour and Lord. What happens after that is of minor importance for none of us is injured by what people think about us. To be a true Christian means that we live by the ideals Christ would give us as the pattern for our lives. This means an attitude to and a way of daily living that must be distinct from the world and those who do not know Christ. While some will think you "peculiar," do not let this disturb you for just as many others will secretly admire you for your stand.

But be sure that you do not assume a sanctimonious attitude to others, or an attitude that you are better than others. Always remember that a Christian is only a sinner saved by grace and that we have no possible cause of boasting or of pride. It is very possible that you will be persecuted by jokes and be misunderstood by some. If you accept this with patience and in a spirit of love, God can use this very thing to help you win some of your friends. Try at all times to show the joy and happiness in your life which a Christian should have. Actually, we are the only people in the world who have a right to be happy for we know where we are now, who is our Saviour, and where we are going. Pray for your friends and love them. God will bless and use you to win them.

I am eighteen years of age, am desperately in love, but my parents don't want me to get married because they say it is too early to know my own mind. They want me to finish my education, but I think love is greater than knowledge. What do you advise?

I have no doubt that you are in love, for love comes to the young as well as the mature. But I think your parents have a point and I think you should pray over this decision which can make or break your life.

The young person who takes a dim view of education is really curtailing his future earning power, and while I have heard of people saying they could live on love, I know of no documented record of anyone ever having done it.

What's wrong with going on to school and staying in love? True love can be a real stimulus to study and a moral balance wheel. After all, it has been the inspiration of some of our great literature, art, and music.

But you must remember that there are two kinds of love. First, there is physical magnetism which is the natural attraction of two people of opposite sex. Then, there is true love which has a spiritual basis. If your love is genuine, it can wait awhile. The Bible says: "Love suffereth long and is kind . . . seeketh not her own." Above all, make sure that you have the mind and will of Christ. Then your decision will be the proper one.

I'm all mixed up and I know it. I am a senior in high school and run with a gang. We have tried everything—and I mean everything—and I know I am going to hell. My mother was a Christian but she is dead and my father is busy and away most of the time. I don't want to live like this and I am afraid to die like this but I feel like I am chained to the devil. What can I do?

Your address is not clear and I cannot write you a personal letter. You have reached the place where you know you are a sinner, are sorry you are a sinner and want help. Strange as it may sound you are on good ground because Christ wants to help and save you but He cannot help the self-sufficient and proud. You feel like you are chained to the devil, but Christ is stronger than the devil, and will release you from his power. Please do just as I say: get in some quiet place and kneel down and tell Jesus all about your troubles. Tell Him about those things you have been doing with the gang—all of them. Tell Him you are sorry but that you keep on doing them. Ask Him to forgive you and to come and live in your heart and give you the power to overcome the temptations you face every day. Then, thank Him for hearing you and being your Saviour and from right then talk to Him any time during the day or night. The question will soon come as to whether you should commit some sin. Stop right then and ask Him to help you. Ask Him whether the place you are going is a place He can go with you. Ask Him if the thing you are planning to do is something He will be with you while you are doing it. Get a Bible right away and start reading it. I would suggest that you take the Gospel of John, in the New Testament, and read it straight through. Then read it again. Then read it again. Ask God to speak to you through the Bible and ask His help to do what it tells you to do. Also, turn to the Old Testament and start reading the Book of Proverbs, one chapter each day. Do this for many months. If you will do this I can promise you your heart will be filled with joy and peace.

My parents have forbidden me to go out with a certain boy. He isn't a bad boy, but very popular in our school. They are objecting to his religion which is different from ours. I don't intend to marry him, but just like the fun of having someone to go with. Shall I defy them and go with him, seeing they are just narrow?

Your parents may seem narrow by present-day standards, but they are far more aware of the subtle dangers of infatuation than you may be. They have observed the many failures that have followed such matches that didn't seem to begin as a serious affair at all. Human emotions are strong, and they sometimes blur our judgment and make it difficult, if not impossible, to make sound judgments.

After you have made allowances for their narrowness, as you call it, and after you have weighed the possibilities, I think you will recognize the wisdom of their directions. Above all, don't defy them. You are still dearly beloved by them, and there is only one chance in a thousand that they are deliberately trying to limit your happiness or impair your chances for future joys. When the Lord gave the Ten Commandments, He told children, "Obey your parents." God who both knows and cares has not ruled this arbitrarily.

My mother died a few years ago, and since then I have kept the home for my father. I want to go on to college and be on my own, but it means breaking up the home. Do I have a Christian responsibility to stay with my father, or should I make the break now?

Not knowing all the elements involved in your decision, I'm afraid I can't give a clear answer. However, you are not bound to maintain a home for your father as a Christian responsibility. Many times people take unfair advantage and this appears to be such a case.

On the other hand, before you leave, you should be certain your father understands and has adequate care. You see, the Christian child has a double responsibility to give honor and respect to the parents. At the same time, the Bible does teach that some of the outstanding examples of Godliness were those who cared for parents in a special way such as Ruth cared for Naomi and was blessed for it. Urge your father to consider with you Ephesians 6:1 and together find God's will. Then you will both find happiness.

I am a teen-ager, and if you know anything about teen-agers you know that we are what many people think of us—mixed-up kids. My problem is that my mind is always full of evil thoughts. Even though I am somewhat active in church and believe like you do concerning Jesus Christ, yet I don't seem to be able to overcome this one great problem.

It is not necessarily true that all teen-agers are "mixed-up kids," even though some of them are. In fact, some adults are still mixed up. The problem you have, however, is one that is shared by many other people, both young and old; and we must turn to the Bible itself to get the answer to this problem. The answer is given in Philippians 4:4–8.

There are several things here that the Christian is told to do. First, we are to rejoice. To do that, you need only to think of the great things God has done for you. Second, we are told not to be anxious, but in our prayers to make our requests known to God. In your biggest problems, you have One whom you can go to; and before Him you can pour out your heart with the assurance that He will not leave you without an answer to that great problem.

Finally, we are to fill our minds with those things that are good. They are mentioned in the Scriptures as being things that are true, honorable, just, pure, lovely, of good report, and of virtue. It is upon these things that we are to think. You can only do this if you follow the admonition found in Colossians 3:16 where the Word of God says: "Let the word of Christ dwell in you richly in all wisdom, teaching and admonishing one another in psalms and hymns and spiritual songs; singing with grace in your hearts unto God." The answer to your question, then, is to live positively, not negatively. Once you learn that secret, God will have given you the victory.

In our high school class are a bunch of really swell kids, and I'd like to run with them. But the only ones who ever ask me to go out are the crumbs. What can I do to get into the other group I like so much?

From your letter, it seems that because you didn't get started with the right group, you did accept the friendship of the other. When you did that you made the mistake you will find hard to correct. Now the really good kids think you have chosen the other crowd to run with them.

Life is full of those situations where you have to make a complete break with the past and start all over again. You have one thing in your favor, you are young, and it's much easier than when you are grown. Even if the high school crowd won't let you change friends, you have your life before you. You are learning many things now, and it would be wise to learn this lesson also.

The greatest and most important change you could make would be to decide for Jesus Christ. By doing so you would close the door on your past and make a new beginning. Then you might not belong to either the socially top group or the leftovers. You would discover a new circle of friends, because you have found the best friend anyone can have, the Lord Jesus Christ.

I know a boy in his early twenties who says he doesn't believe in heaven or hell, and says the Bible is a fairy tale. He is real sweet, and was raised in a Christian home but still thinks this way. How can I change his way of thinking?

It is not too unusual for persons in their early twenties to defect from their early teaching. The reasons are many. Perhaps his exposure to unbelief "took" better than his exposure to belief. This is often the case, for the Bible says: "The heart of man is deceitful above all things." The human heart is as prepared by sin to accept unbelief as faith. Some person he regards very highly has undoubtedly influenced his thinking, and for the time being he looks on his early training as "bunk." As someone once said, "A little learning may take a man away from God, but full understanding will bring him back." Some of the stanchest Christians I know are people who had periods in their life when they questioned the Bible, Christ, and God. But as they continued to examine the matter, there was overwhelming evidence that "only the fool hath said in his heart, there is no God."

How can you change his way of thinking? This will have to be the work of God. You can pray for him, and reason with him, but don't argue. What you *are* will be much more convincing than what you say.

Lately I have dated a boy, but I have a funny feeling about him. I just broke a date for next Saturday night, for I have a fear of the crowd he runs with. Was I right in doing this?

I am happy to hear from a girl who will listen to the voice of intuition and conscience. It is one of woman's greatest gifts, and I wish that more of them would exercise it, rather than yield to their emotions.

It is sometimes better to break your date than to ruin your life. I imagine some of those New York girls who were with the boys who murdered their rivals recently wish they had listened to their consciences and stayed home. They are in serious trouble.

There are enough fine, wholesome young men to date. I don't think any girl should date anyone she is afraid of. When a boy shows tendencies to be tough and violent, he should be avoided like a person who has the plague. It is sad that many boys who are beset with feelings of inferiority think they must impress the opposite sex by brandishing knives, or other deadly weapons.

It has always taken more courage to be good than to be bad. And I admire your good judgment in breaking a date with a boy who shows tendencies of violence. If all girls would do this, perhaps boys would learn to stand on their own two feet, rather than lean on the mass strength of a "gang."

I am a high school boy and though I am a Christian, I feel left out when I don't go with the gang. They do things that I don't think are right, but somehow I don't have the courage to go on my own. Is there something wrong with my Christian life and experience?

Everyone feels the need of belonging, and there is nothing morally wrong in wanting to be accepted by your classmates.

But you say the "gang" does things that you don't think are right, and that puts the picture in a different frame. Many a youth is behind prison bars today simply because he didn't want to be called "chicken." And every boy who considers acceptance by the "gang" more important than his inner sense of right and wrong is headed for trouble.

As a Christian, which you say you are, you must remember that it is better to associate yourself with a good little gang than a big, bad one. In history Christians have often been found in the minority, and those men who have had the strength to stand alone have been the men who have influenced history and made the world a better place to live in. There is nothing wrong with your Christian life if you will just give it a chance to grow. But many a rose has withered and died in a weed patch. It takes some doing to develop Christian character, but it's worth it.

Daniel stood alone in Babylon . . . Joseph stood alone in Egypt. You may have to stand alone, but you won't be alone . . . Christ will be with you.

My parents make me go to Sunday school, but they don't go themselves. To make it worse, the Sunday school teacher is never prepared and just reads out of the quarterly. Are my parents right in making me go?

No, your parents are not right, and neither is the Sunday school teacher. Too long, parents have just sent children to Sunday school, when they should go with them. Too long Sunday school teachers have read from the quarterly.

I am sure that you can see the problem clearer than your parents can. Why don't you begin to urge them to go with you? They must know that it is a good thing to do. Then they will see how poorly some Sunday schools are run, and they may do something to correct it.

Above all, don't blame God or Christianity for what some people do. Think of Sunday school as it should be, and the Lord may even use you to bring about a change. Pray for His help, and don't be discouraged. The great prophet, Samuel, was only a child when God spoke to Israel through him (I Samuel 3:1). Let God use you rather than letting the devil tempt you to failure and defeat.

I am a teen-age high-schooler. I just learned that I am the child of unmarried parents, and I am almost desperate with grief. I wish I were dead. Do you think it's such a terrible thing for me to be such a child?

It is a very unhappy thing for you to know that your parents are such people. They have not given you the start you should have. But you should not feel so terribly about it. The wrong was theirs and not yours. God will never hold such a thing against you, and you don't need to tell people about it.

One of the miracles about becoming a Christian is that no part of our past is held against us. God not only forgives the sins of our lives, but He completely forgets every one of them. When He accepts you into the family, He makes a new person out of you, and none of the things that now seem so important are carried over. All God wants from you now is your complete reliance upon the merit of His son to save you, and your utter abandonment to His will. The change is as complete as if you had died and then been raised again. That is what the Bible means when it says: "We were buried therefore with Him by Baptism into death: that like as Christ was raised from the dead through the glory of God the Father, so we also might walk in newness of life" (Romans 6:4).

In our high school, there is a girl who follows me and calls me all sweet names. My parents say I should be nice to her because I am a Christian, but when I am nice to her, she just clings to me. Can you suggest a course of action for me as a Christian?

This girl friend of yours appears to have some of the symptoms of sexual abnormality. She can be dangerous if encouraged too much, and therefore your problem is a difficult one. If you know what her problem is, you can be on guard against undue familiarity. At the same time, you may be able to help her.

Many times, Christians make the mistake of thinking that they cannot help people spiritually unless they become intimate in their conversation and very confidential. That is not our calling as witnesses. Be careful in all your dealings with her to be very frank and open in your witness, but do not commit yourself to her under any conditions. Be careful not to win her to yourself and fail to win her to Christ. He can help her, but you cannot. The Bible says: "He that winneth souls is wise," not just wise because he wins them but he wins them because he is wise (Proverbs 11:30).

My mother has forbidden me to indulge in petting when I go out with boys. All the kids do it, and don't you think she is just old-fashioned?

Petting is one of the major problems for the teen-ager today. Because it is so generally done, I am not surprised that a Christian young person should wonder about it. One time Jesus said that "Because iniquity shall abound, the love of the many shall become cold." We become so accustomed to wrong practices, and growing used to it makes it seem less of an evil. You could have asked any competent doctor or physiologist and they would have told you that petting is the preliminary act to the sex relation. To excite oneself when satisfaction is neither safe nor right is harmful to your constitution and to your mental life as well. It is known that there are times when young persons are unable to control themselves once excited. If those who counsel this way do so from the physiological and psychological point of view, I am sure that the Christian young person would not want to jeopardize his spiritual victory and his effective witness for a brief moment of unsatisfactory excitement.

I have committed a horrible sin and I want to know if it means that I must go to hell. I am only fifteen years old but have committed adultery with a married man. Is it possible for God to forgive me when I really don't repent of my sins?

The Bible clearly teaches that before we receive forgiveness from our sins, there must be sincere repentance. The sin you have committed is a very serious one, because you have entered into a relationship that is one of the most sacred of all relationships in life.

Many times adultery is condemned in the Bible, and this is the Christian standard. Under the law of Moses its punishment was death (Leviticus 20:10, Deuteronomy 22:22–24). As serious as this sin may be, God can forgive it. Read John 8:3–11, but do not forget that without repentance there is no hope of forgiveness. Repentance will mean more than sorrow for sin. It will mean that with God's help you renounce it once and for all.

I am the oldest child in our family. I have to do most of the work, and Dad and Mother just spoil the other kids. I can't help feeling resentful and mean. Can you help me in any way to understand this problem?

Being the oldest child naturally imposes a responsibility upon you. You will find in life that as we grow older we must shoulder greater responsibility. This is all part of growing up.

You say you can't help feeling resentful and mean. With this I can't agree. Resentment grows with practice just like patience grows with practice. It takes effort to develop bad character, just as it takes effort to develop good character.

Accept your lot in life like a man. Throw your shoulders back and say, "I will do my work, even if the other children don't." And above all, take God as a partner in life. Christ has a way of making burdens which seem unbearable, light. "Take My yoke upon you, and learn of Me," He said, "for My yoke is easy and My burden is light."

I was recently elected to be president of my class in high school. Many of the traditional activities I cannot take part in as a Christian. Do you think it wise for me to resign or continue in office?

You will have to make your own decisions all through life concerning doubtful practices. The office itself does not entail an activity you disapprove. It does put you in a place where you can bear a most effective witness to Christ. You are never responsible for activities the rest call for, for you have been chosen to preside and guide but not to require them to do certain things. As long as you are able, take a clear position without compromise, let the office be a vantage point from which to proclaim the gospel method with tact and force. Jesus said that the apostles should be "wise as serpents and harmless as doves." Do your work well and gain the admiration and respect of your class, and they in turn will accept your Christian influence. As the "salt of the earth" we must go everywhere with the message of Christ.

I am a young girl who is very mixed up. I don't know if I'm a Christian or not. You see, my mother is one of the leaders in the church and father is on the board. But here at home they quarrel all the time. They sometimes don't stop until I cry. Are they Christians?

It would be better, of course, if I could hear your mother's and father's side of the story. Teen-agers are often great idealists, and they sometimes interpret any little family discussion as "quarreling." But let us assume that your mother and father do quarrel, as you say they do. This, of course, would be very distressing to you, and might cause you to question your mother's and father's religious sincerity.

But as you grow older you will find that sometimes otherwise good people have dispositional weaknesses, and that little personality clashes are part and parcel of life. As an idealist, you have a golden opportunity of helping your parents. The Bible says: "And a little child may lead them." Since your parents stop their bickering when you cry, this shows that they respect you and your convictions. I think that you could quietly discuss this matter with them, and as you prayerfully work together on this problem, I feel sure that conditions in the home can be improved. Children are often the cause of parental disagreements. Just make sure that you don't contribute to the situation by selfish attitudes. The Bible says: "Let nothing be done through strife or vainglory: but in lowliness of mind let each esteem others better than themselves."

Do you think it is right for parents to try to force their children to accept their religion? My father and mother always say that if it's good enough for my parents it's good enough for me.

Your parents might be right providing they have embraced the truth in their religion, but if they have not, then their religion is not good enough for them or for you. In fact, religion can never be forced upon anyone. The very nature of true religion is that it is voluntary. Every person must make his own free choice when all the information is in possession. Christianity is promoted by instruction and example. Truths must be understood and to be understood they must be embodied in persons who believe.

But give your parents the benefit of the doubt. They may be nothing more than overly zealous, and in their zeal to have you discover the truth, they may use the wrong method. Perhaps you have had opportunities they never had, so give their views prayerful consideration; compare them with the teaching of the Bible, and then you will be in a position to decide such questions on your own with the help of God. "As many as received Him, to them gave He the right to become the children of God, even to those that believed on His name."

I live in a fraternity house and am a Christian. There are some things going on which I would very much like to change. How can I accomplish this? I feel so much alone.

Turn to your Bible and read the wonderful stories of men who were alone in godless surroundings but who, by the help and presence of the living God, made a marvelous contribution to their own times. Joseph was surrounded by sin and intrigue in Egypt. His master's wife tried to seduce him. He was tested by imprisonment, but through it all he trusted in God and sought to know and do His will, and he stands today as a wonderful example of the keeping and strengthening power of God in the heart of a man who believed in Him.

Daniel and his companions were tempted to forsake their godly heritage, but they refused. They even faced a fiery furnace rather than compromise. God honored their faith and mightily used them. Moses was surrounded by the luxury and godlessness of the Egyptian court but cast in his lot with his own people. Lot lived in Sodom and saw the obscenities of that doomed city. God saved him out of it because he trusted in Him. Every one of our Lord's apostles sealed their faith with their lives. Since then history has been replete with the lives of men who have put God and His way of life above all else. I do not know the particular problems which you face in your fraternity house but I would urge you to pray daily that God will give you the love, patience, wisdom, and Christian grace to witness for Him and to live as a Christian should live. There is tremendous power in the influence of one man completely devoted to knowing and doing God's will.

I have been raised in an atmosphere where social drinking has been taken as a matter of course. My daughter is showing signs of becoming addicted to liquor. What is the Christian solution?

I am sorry for you and am thankful that you are desperately worried. Your problem is being reflected in thousands of American homes today. Alcoholism is increasing by leaps and bounds. It is now being considered as a disease and the emphasis seems to be on teaching people how to drink in moderation. As I see it, under present conditions, there is but one safe and Christian solution—total abstinence. Liquor is not necessary either for health or for so-called gracious living. On the other hand, it is the cause of untold sorrow, suffering and material loss, not to mention the spiritual implications of drinking. In the Bible, in the Book of Proverbs, we read these words: "Wine is a mocker, strong drink is raging: and whosoever is deceived thereby is not wise." These words were written nearly three thousand years ago but they are true today. In America it seems to be a peculiar problem—Americans seem unusually lacking in judgment or restraint about liquor. During the war, one of our leading officials said that the gravest danger to America centered in the cocktail lounges in Washington. Liquor loosens tongues and removes inhibitions and can do infinite harm. As to your daughter, ask God to help her and set out on a program immediately whereby you try to undo the harm already done and lead her to Christ who will give her the victory over her desire.

I am the child of separated parents. I would like to live with my mother who is a Christian, but the courts have ruled that I must live with my father. I don't like to live with him, but what can I do?

Legally, until you have reached the age of responsibility, you must abide by the ruling of the court. Every broken home situation is an unhappy one, and especially trying for the children. This situation is not an easy one for you. Many young people become rebellious and defiant to make up for their unhappiness. This will accomplish nothing for you.

When you have no alternative, it is always best to accept graciously whatever your lot may be. Do not make your father and yourself miserable over the decision of the court. In fact, this may be God's way of bringing your own father to the Saviour. Love him as your father, and witness to him as one who needs Christ. Even though he is not a believer, you still have the Bible admonition to honor him as your earthly father.

Above all, learn to be contented with the things that you have, for the Bible says: "Be content with such things as ye have, for He Himself hath said, I will in no wise fail thee, neither will I in any wise forsake thee" (Hebrews 13:5).

I am only a young fellow, but my faith in Jesus is very real. Neither my father nor mother are Christians, and they won't let me go to the church I like. They would rather have me stay home than go there. Sometimes I sneak out, but then it bothers me. Should I sneak out anyhow to hear God's Word preached?

Your parents are unreasonable, for they are refusing to permit you to do the one thing that will make you become a son they can be justly proud of. Their eyes are blinded by Satan, and they cannot see their big mistake. The Bible says that "And even if our gospel is hid, it is hid to them that are lost: in whom the God of this world hath blinded the minds of them which believe not" (II Corinthians 4:3-4). Don't become discouraged and irritated over this. Your parents need your prayers and example. Sometimes parents can lead their children to Christ, but many times children have brought their own parents to the Saviour.

In answer to your question, I would say: go every chance you have to hear the gospel, listen to it on the radio, read your Bible and some good Christian literature. But in the home be an example of a Christian by being obedient, even when they are unreasonable.

Chapter 5

What Every Parent Should Know

Our sixteen-year-old son is rebellious and we are afraid h
will become a problem to us. My husband and I both work
Can you recommend some place where we can send him so
he will be properly managed?

There is no substitute for a home for a sixteen-year-old boy
Many of our finest young people are presently rebelling
against neglect more than anything else. They need the sense
of security that comes from a home where they are loved
and wanted. They need the discipline of a well-ordered home
to prepare them for social obligations as adults. It would be
far better for you to adjust your scale of living to a smaller
budget, and have the necessary time to give to your young
son. In a short time he will be leaving home. Then you will
forever regret that you did not give him the home training
for which there is no good substitute. Teach him the basic
principles of good character. Teach him eternal values. Help
him to find his way to God as he observes your life and your
walk with God. You have the solution to your problem within
reach. Do not neglect it while you have opportunity. And remember there is no substitute for love.

My thirteen-year-old daughter has started lying to the extent
where I cannot believe anything she says. She has now started

smoking and is losing all her friends. However, her grades are very good and she attends Sunday school and church. Could you please help me?

I can well understand your being disturbed by your daughter's behavior. She is entering those difficult years where she is neither child nor adult. In her desire to appear grown-up she is taking on some of the less admirable adult characteristics. This is caused by a lack of security, and it is at this stage where she needs love and understanding more than at any other period of her life.

She also needs guidance and example. Make sure that you set a stable example before her. I think it would be a good thing if you could sit down and discuss these things with her. And if you have failed her at any point, you be honest and confess your shortcomings too. You never mentioned whether or not she has made a commitment to Christ. She is at the age where she needs the strength that comes from a living, vital faith. Many children become lost to the home and to society at this age. But it is also the ideal age to make a Christian commitment. Urge your daughter to do this, and if you have been remiss in your Christian life, it would be wonderful for mother and daughter to begin a new spiritual adventure with Christ.

I am the mother of two young boys who find their greatest joy in watching television. Unhappily, they see more than their share of violence. Is there any device we can use to counteract this growing menace to our youth?

You can be sure that the producers of television programs do not care to force any kind of program on the viewing and listening public. They want to attract the largest number so that the advertising is more effective. In other words, they give what the public demands. As long as the majority will accept violence pictures they will be shown. Such portrayals are the easiest to produce and call for the least effort and dramatic ability.

You can protest directly to the station and get as many

others as you can to do the same. You can also commence those who send the finer programs into your home. It is time that the Christian voice was heard on this matter. Jesus said "Ye are the salt of the earth" and as such He intended that we should lend our influence to the greatest possible extent He also said, "Ye are the light of the world," and as such have a God-given responsibility for disseminating true light on every question as well as giving witness to our personal faith.

Also you must teach your children "choice" in their TV watching. There are many programs we just don't allow our children to see. In fact, we limit their watching to one or two a day, and those only under our supervision.

My daughter is about to marry a man who is not a Christian I feel that I must stop their marriage, but don't know what I can do about it. Should I just show her where the Bible forbids such marriages?

Isn't it a little late for you to begin to instruct your daughter about such things? I'm afraid that there is very little you can do now, for no matter what you do, it will be construed as interference. You should have taught her the Christian view of marriage before she had any prospects of marriage, for then she would have been able to make a wise decision.

The Bible teaches that "The aged women be reverent in demeanor not slanderess nor enslaved to much wine, teachers of that which is good; that they may train young women to love their husbands, to love their children, to be chaste, workers at home, kind, being in subjection to their own husbands that the word of God be not blasphemed" (Titus 2:3–5).

Had you fulfilled your responsibility when your daughter was growing, you would not have that problem now. There are some things in life that cannot be undone, and although the Lord will forgive every sin, we must often live with the problems we created before we came to the Saviour.

Yet, I would suggest that you have a heart-to-heart talk with her—then have prayer with her. Commit it to God. He can change the situation even at this late date.

We have been keeping our children out of release-time re-
ligious instruction in the schools because we don't agree with
the teaching they receive. Are we doing the right thing to
compel them to be so different?

To the children, it is a serious thing to be compelled to be
different. Do you know how many others do not attend the
religious training program? Perhaps they are not so different.
I would suggest a principle by which to judge your decisions.
First, avoid making it a matter of discipline if possible. Do
not put the children in a position where they become rebellious. I do not believe the teaching will harm them, for
there are very few people who will freely give their time unless they have some interest in the children. Second, you
should be well informed as to the teaching they receive.
Make sure that it is according to the Scriptures and the historic Christian faith. It will take some effort on your part,
but this is your responsibility. Third, take an active part in
school affairs so that you can exert Christian influence to off-
set erroneous teaching. Finally, use this study to teach your
children how to distinguish truth from error and how to
make their own decisions and not always follow any teaching.

I am a widower with two teen-age daughters. They are not
bad but I am active in church and believe in complete sep-
aration from the world and my daughters are a bit unruly.
What can I do?

Are you separated from the world or separated to some pious
opinions which may not stand the test of our Lord's scrutiny?
I do not mean to sound harsh for I know you have a difficult
problem. But, be very sure that the separation about which
you talk is that which is truly Christian. Some of the most
unattractive Christians in the world are those who have
built a fence of prohibitions around themselves and keep
most people outside the fence. Remember that teen-age girls
are full of life and need to have a happy time. Be sure that
the Christianity you profess does not repel them because it
is long-faced and full of "don'ts." I would not imply for one

minute that there are not many things Christians should not do. Of the Ten Commandments, most of them are commandments against specific sins. But, it is very easy for older people to expand these prohibitions to things which are in themselves perfectly all right. I have on my desk a letter from a boy who enjoys wrestling at the YMCA. His mother thinks it is dangerous and unbecoming of a Christian. She is making the mistake of confusing wholesome exercise and recreation with sinful pleasures. Try to avoid this, enter into the happiness of these young lives in your home. Make Christianity a joyful experience. Above all, ask God for daily guidance in your task.

Chapter 6

After the Children Are Grown

Recently I have become troubled over the fact that my daughter does not confide in me. Right now I know she is planning marriage, but has not told me. Shall I insist on her telling me such things or shall I wait?

If you have lost the confidence of your daughter, it is almost too late to regain it. You have forgotten that she has been growing up and is an adult. You have probably treated her and her problems as being unimportant or as you did when she was a child. Parents lose the full confidence of their children through a lack of sympathy and understanding more than anything else. Most likely you forgot to be interested in her growing love for the man she intends to marry, and you probably forgot that he was becoming a man and no longer a boy. If you can make her understand that you are interested in her problems without becoming a judge and critic, you might regain some of the trust you have lost. It is too late to instruct a young woman about the choice of a husband when she falls in love. It must be done before then. Then don't forget that in our frequent human failures, we can always call upon the Lord for special wisdom and understanding. God is concerned with your problems and if you desire all things to be for His glory, He can undo for you something that has been done.

We have a seventeen-year-old daughter who has fallen in love with a low-type fellow, and she insists that she is going

to marry him. Our hearts will be broken if she weds beneath
her class. Can you tell us what to do?

May I remind you that there are two things that parents
often have little control over, especially after they happen.
We have little control over our children's falling in love.
Second, we often have little control over whom they fall
in love with. I can well understand your distress of mind,
but let us examine your question a bit and see if perhaps
you are not jumping at conclusions.

First of all, what do you mean by a "low-type" fellow?
Do you mean that he lives on the "wrong side of the tracks"?
Do you regret this affair just because he is of a different
social status than your family? Sometimes even princes and
kings marry commoners. The prince of the royal family
of Japan married a tradesman's daughter, and everyone
seemed happy about it. It seems to me that you are more
concerned that your daughter marry "in her class" than
you are about the character of this young man. You should
be more concerned about his being a Christian, and whether
he is honest and understanding. I know many young men
with social standing who would make poor husbands.

On the other hand, your daughter seems a bit young to
be thinking of marriage. You should counsel her to be sure
this is God's choice for her life—also encourage her to
wait at least two years. This time period may help you
and her.

My daughter married a man I never liked. I do not approve
of him, and he is hateful to me. What can be done in a
situation like this?

The young man is now your son-in-law. You must accept
him as your daughter's husband. The choice was made by
your daughter, and if you love her you must accept her
choice, otherwise you will be separated from her. You must
accept him in love and understanding. You have no other
choice except to lose your daughter's affection. Keep your
prejudices to yourself. Pray that they may be happy. Perform little acts of helpfulness and kindliness for the young

folks. If you accept Christ and then lead your young people to Him, an unlikely person as you believe your son-in-law to be can become the best of men.

My husband and I have been Christians for many years. We have a daughter who is past thirty years and is still at home with us. She helps around the house but has no plans for the future. What is our responsibility?

Evidently she has not learned that some time we must all assume the role of an adult and accept responsibility. No doubt your Christian kindness and consideration have been outstanding but you have failed in discipline, at least in some areas. I think a very direct talk with her, in the presence of your pastor or someone she respects. Make it clear that you have fulfilled your part of the responsibility in preparing her for life but that she must make a decision to step out on her own with the help of the Lord. Her problem is one of a lack of self-confidence. If you can give her such confidence in her God-given talents and in the guidance and provision of God, you will help her win one of life's great battles. The longer she tarries, the more difficult the break will be. An easy transition would be to secure employment away from home for a time and then be completely on her own. Perhaps she is too concerned about what you will do without her. Assure her that you can manage.

I have two grown-up sons. One of my daughters-in-law has a terribly jealous and possessive nature. She resents our son coming to visit us and scarcely ever allows us to see their child. This is a great grief to my husband and myself. What can we do?

The key to this unhappy situation really lies in the hands of your son. In my opinion he ought to have taken a firm hand in the matter at the start and not to have allowed his wife to dictate to him in this matter.

The Bible teaches that the husband is the head of the wife and that the wife is to be in subjection to her husband (Ephesians 5:22, 23). In the case of your son and daughter-in-law, the positions seem to have got reversed.

It is unfortunate that your son should ever have married a woman of this antisocial type; but since nothing can alter that now, I can only advise you to point out to him how keenly you and your husband feel the situation and urge him to assert his authority in his own home.

At the same time you will not, I am sure, wish to impose any strain on his relations with his wife or create friction between them. Maybe he is happy with this woman, and I hope the child is also happy and well cared for.

As you have opportunity, show to your daughter-in-law all possible kindness and consideration. Let her feel that you have no desire to take her husband and child from her and be on your guard lest a jealous and possessive spirit should spoil your own life. Pray that the love of God may break all barriers down and unite you all in love for Him and one another.

I am a Christian widow and mother of seven children. My daughter has married a man who has been married three times before. I feel that she walked into sin with her eyes open. Can I allow him to come to my house, and should I accept him into my home and heart? How can I do this?

You didn't mention the circumstances surrounding this man's previous marriages, but we will assume that he is a divorcé. There are three things that I would like to say to you in regard to this situation:

First, the die is cast—your daughter is married to this man, and whatever you do can't change that. It is probably not the situation you had wanted for your daughter, but unfortunately we parents cannot always plan our children's lives.

Second, it is possible that this man has never had contact with a real Christian. You must give him that privilege, and it is altogether possible that you may be able to lead him to Christ, if you try. He has probably suffered a great deal in his many marriages, and stands in need of the strength and forgiveness Christ can give.

Third, it is not Christian to shun sinners. Jesus ate with publicans and sinners, and we are not nearly as good as Him. By all means, treat him kindly, and it is possible that you can help him and your daughter to build a Christian home.

Please advise me in this difficulty. I am a Christian, a widow, and my son who is finishing his residency in surgery has decided to go as a medical missionary. Should I try to keep him from wasting his life and talents?

You should be thankful to God that you have a son who has felt the call to the mission field. Far from wasting his life and talents, he will be using them probably as he could never do in this country. It has been my privilege to visit many mission fields and I have found that missionaries are the finest ambassadors America has abroad. But, far more important, Christian missionaries are taking the message of Christ and His love and saving grace to peoples who need it, just as we do in America. Christ tells us that "whosoever will save his life shall lose it; but whosoever will lose his life for My sake, the same shall save it." By this He means that a life spent for self is a wasted life while one spent for others is one spent according to His will. I can well realize that you anticipate separation from your son with a great sense of loss. Let me urge you to consider it an honor that he feels God's call to serve on the mission field. He will not make much money but he will help people who otherwise will not be helped, and best of all, he will tell them of the Christ Who alone is the hope of the world. I once met a missionary who was living in primitive conditions and working under most adverse circumstances. But he was one of the happiest people I have ever met. He was following God's will for his life and God was using him to win souls to Christ. That is the greatest joy in this world.

Chapter 7

Solving Problems on the Job

Is it always right to tell the truth, especially when you know it will hurt someone? If I tell the truth about my business affairs, it will ruin chances for the happiness of my family.

I would rather answer you by stating the matter in quite another way. It is always wrong to be dishonest. Dishonesty is never justified. God will never approve, and even your own conscience will rise up to condemn you sooner or later. I have not known of a single instance when a man has been ruined or his family injured because of his basic honesty. It may not always be either wise or expedient to announce publicly all of your personal affairs, but to conceal the truth from persons involved is never the right course of action.

If you had been sure of the matter, you would never have raised the question. The Bible says: "But he that doubteth is condemned if he eat, because he eateth not of faith; and whatsoever is not of faith is sin." Do nothing until all the doubts are removed. This is a fairly safe procedure in all matters.

In my work as an accountant I am constantly in knowledge of the dishonesty of those who work in this organization. It doesn't involve my work in any way, but how can I be silent about it and still know that it is going on?

Recently the American people have been told of the largest swindle in history. It is the daily dishonest practices of men in business of all kinds, making use of legitimate channels to increase their income at the expense of the company. If such men held up a bank or store at the point of a gun, would you report it? I'm sure you would regard it as an act of a good citizen. Once when the children of Israel were being plundered, the Edomites stood by and watched, but gave no aid nor reported it. God said: "For the violence done to thy brother, shame shall cover thee, and thou shalt be cut off forever. In the day that thou stoodest on the other side, in the day when strangers carried away his substance, and foreigners entered into his gates, and cast lots upon Jerusalem, even thou wast one of them" (Obadiah 1:10-11). Thus God held a people responsible because they, knowing, watched and did not protest against evil being done. You have a responsibility you cannot shirk and maintain a clear conscience.

I am a partner in a small manufacturing concern. Due to business reverses we have been forced into bankruptcy. When the people of my church learned that I had filed bankruptcy, they insisted upon dropping me from the membership. Was my action so wrong that I can no longer have the fellowship with Christians?

That depends entirely upon the reasons and upon the motives of bankruptcy. Personal bankruptcy in order to avoid the payment of just debts is certainly not honest and not Christian. However, even men in the world of business recognize that there is a legitimate cause for bankruptcy when it is intended to avert law suits and litigation, in order to give you opportunity to make good debts that have been honestly incurred. People unfamiliar with the procedure of business are not able to detect what your motives are. You will, however, have to give an answer to the Lord. Our prayer for you will be that your reason was to glorify Christ by being honest in all of your relations and this was merely a method to accomplish that in the least possible time. Meanwhile, do not condemn the people of your church for their action. They simply did not understand your reasons and acted most likely according to the best light they had.

I have a job in an office which is so large and in which there is so little supervision that some of the girls do practically nothing all day long. They say they are "riding the gravy train" and got mad when I said they were stealing. What is right?

The acceptance of pay for which a corresponding service is not rendered is dishonest. I think, from what you write, that you are correct in saying these girls are stealing. But I am not sure you have approached the problem in a way to help. If you are a Christian, your first obligation is to see that you yourself give a full day's work for your wages. Then, as opportunity presents itself, you can wisely bring up the discussion of what is right and what is wrong. If such a discussion is started in a proper spirit, some of these girls may be led to be more faithful in their work. If all tactful methods fail, it would not be unethical to suggest to the head of the office force that some system of supervision be set up to insure more effective work by all. One of the Ten Commandments is "Thou shalt not steal." There are many ways of taking that which is not our own. Many of us have been guilty of failing to do all that we could to earn that which we are paid. Make this problem a matter of prayer. See if there are not other Christian girls in the office and ask them to join in praying about it. Above all, do not assume a holier-than-thou attitude. Be sure you are living as a Christian, not only in relation to your office work but also in other ways.

I am one of the policemen who was converted in one of your meetings. The other night I caught a young man involved in a crime and led him to a personal faith. He promised to go straight, and I didn't turn him in. Was I wrong in this and did I fail in my duty?

You are to be commended for speaking directly to the spiritual needs of the young man. It is always thrilling to hear of policemen who are witnessing for Christ. You did more than catch a criminal and punish him. You were used by God to change his life.

But he must have wronged someone in the crime, and you are given the duty to protect such persons. Since I do not know all the details, you may have acted within your right as a law-enforcement officer, but it does not seem wise to dismiss such a person. After coming to Christ, the young man should have been made to see that he has a debt to society. Even God does not let the sinner go scot-free. Christ had to bear the penalty of our sins in order for us to be forgiven. While you have done a wonderful thing in leading him to Christ, it is possible that you have been guilty of a misjudgment.

I am a clerk in a small-town bank. I have reason to believe that the cashier is dishonest. I am afraid to report him lest I lose my position, yet I believe it should be checked on. What is my responsibility in a case like this?

Your report would never need to be made known. The bank examiners would appreciate any information and it would be kept in strictest confidence. You have a higher responsibility than to a dishonest employer. You are a servant of the community and you have a responsibility to them. To remain silent would be to participate in the crime just as much as we sin when we give assent to the sin of others. The Christian has a great obligation to be ethical and honest in all things, even sometimes at personal hazard. It is in the difficult situation that the qualities of a Christian are seen. They may go without notice in normal conditions, but when the crisis comes, then the distinctive qualities of the Christian are clearly seen.

In my business in order to make a profit, we always depend on outwitting our clients and customers. Seeing this is a standard way of conducting this kind of business, do you think it is right for me as a Christian to follow that practice?

For the true Christian, there is no double standard. The ethics of the Christian faith are truly expressed in Luke 3:10 through 14, that nothing less than absolute honesty has the approval of God. The moral collapse of our times is due to the fact that we have based our morals on social custom rather than on the word of God, which alone provides an absolute standard.

The Bible says: "A false balance is abomination to the Lord: but a just weight is His delight" (Proverbs 11:1).

Can a Christian be a member of a labor organization? I have been advised not to join, but unless I do I will continue to be out of work.

The Bible does forbid our being unequally yoked together with unbelievers, but only where that yoke forces us to partake in their wickedness. A labor union as such is not evil. In fact, some of them have had definitely beneficial effects on the entire history of labor and industry.

Today, a few of them have gotten into the hands of unprincipled and unscrupulous men who have brought disrepute on the entire organization. In unions, as in politics, this has happened because men with high standards and Christian convictions have withdrawn and turned the entire movement over to the forces of evil.

Now at last, many good Christians are aware of their former errors and are taking places of responsibility in the world, not willing that wicked men should have the control. Take your place and accept responsibility, but never with the intent of compromise or participation in the evil practices. Commit yourself to Jesus Christ, and then go on to extend the Gospel and Christian standards. Remember that Jesus said: "Ye are the salt of the earth," and also that "Ye are the light of the world." We cannot do our duty unless we invade the world for Christ.

I am a Christian and a worker in the church. I want my life to be an example for the Lord. I work as an accountant for a large business firm. Recently, I was approached by the owner of a large night club and gambling house to become their accountant. I would have the same work I now have with a greatly increased salary. Would you advise such a change?

I do not wonder that you were sought out for such work. Even men who earn their living through dishonest and questionable means appreciate the honesty of the Christian. Certainly this man would like to hire you at such a high salary, for he would no doubt save it by having one he could trust with his money. Although the world may at times laugh at the Christian for his simple faith, it will admire the standards and the lives of those who so believe.

It would be a doubtful change for you to make. Remember, you are not dealing with a person who is possessed of the scruples you appreciate. The increased salary can never compensate for the deadening influence such a place would have on your spiritual life. In the place where you now work, the small salary is still legitimate and justly earned. There are principles that we must hold to maintain a clear conscience. You cannot afford to sacrifice the influence of your life for the questionable increase in salary. Take it as a token of recognition from the world of the sterling qualities of the Christian, and thank God for what He gives you honestly.

I am interested in going into a small business for myself. If I do so, I will be sometimes involved in Sunday work. I would like to have your opinion on the use of Sunday for business purposes.

I wish it would be possible for all of us to reserve Sunday as the Lord's day and as a true Christian Sabbath. This would give free opportunity for everyone to engage in Christian worship and activity. Nothing hinders the progress of the Gospel in and through the church more than the increasing secular use of the Lord's day. If you can do so, you should reserve the one day in seven for unhampered worship and service for Him.

On the other hand, Christians are in constant danger of a legalistic attitude toward Sunday and toward other Christian observances. We must retain the Gospel freedom that has been purchased by Christ. Nothing should be cherished more than our liberty in Christ. We must not submit to a legalistic Christianity that is encumbered with commands and prohibitions. Our first and greatest commandment is to love God and to love our neighbor as ourselves. Therefore, you must make the final decision in this matter. You will ultimately be required to answer to God for the use you make of your money and of your time. I believe you will make no mistake if what you do is done in sincerity that is enlightened through a study of the Bible. Above all, do not allow your proposed business to ever become an obstacle to your devotion and service to Christ.

I am a Christian and am trying to make my life count for God, but I work in an office where racy stories and sexy conversation are in vogue. How can I cope with this without being prudish or appearing "better-than-thou"?

A Christian businessman from Florida who faces a similar problem writes that he has found an effective way to lick this problem. He says that he keeps a New Testament on his desk in plain view of everyone. He says that he has yet to have anyone come into his office who did not respect his "silent reminder" and refrain from profanity or smutty stories.

There are many ways that we can rebuke those who are given to obscenity without being offensive. I find that the average person respects a person with ideals, if we let him know by our manner of life where we stand. As a rule, it is the person they are in doubt about, in whose presence they spill out their filth. So make sure that your testimony is clear, and that your life is of a quality that will inspire respect.

Woodrow Wilson once told the story of a man who used profane language in the presence of the President's father, a Presbyterian minister. "I beg your pardon," the man said to Wilson's father. "Oh sir, you have not offended me," he said. "All profane language is an offense toward Him whose name is profaned."

I am a pupil nurse in a very large hospital. Most of the doctors treat all of us with respect and consideration but one of the most famous surgeons curses before us and makes vile jokes about the nurses working with him. I am a Christian and willing to take anything I should but this seems too much.

It seems to me you have several definite courses of action. Get one or two of your fellow nurses and face this doctor with what he is doing. Ask him if he would be willing to have his own daughter subjected to what you are subjected to. Tell him you will do any work which he requires of you and try to do it faithfully and to the best of your ability but that you will not submit to his actions further. If this does not get the desired results you should report the situation to your superintendent of nurses, and to the hospital administrator, if necessary. It is my understanding that all hospital staffs have a committee which deals with personal problems, where necessary. It may be that you should appeal to this committee. In any case, be sure that you keep your Christian witness clear. You have right on your side so stick to your guns. The Bible says: "The wicked flee when no man pursueth, but the righteous are as bold as a lion."

I am a Christian, a trained office-machine worker, and have a good job. My problem is that all day long I hear talk about things which are either suggestive or downright vulgar. What should I do?

The easy way out, except for losing your job, is to quit. But the easy way is not always the right way. I can advise you but you should do nothing until you have acted on this advice. Make this a matter of definite prayer. God knows the situation and He loves all of those people who are now indulging in vulgar talk. Tell Him you are willing to do whatever He leads you to do, then ask Him to show you what it is. It may be that God will give you the wisdom to talk to these people, not in a prudish way but by saying there are so many good and lovely things to talk about and by helping you to change the general habits of conversation in the office. Let those around you realize that their talk distresses you but be sure you do this with both tact and patience. I know of instances where this very thing has transformed an entire office. Once it happened in a shop where one Christian man was used to change the entire atmosphere of the place. As a Christian, remember that you are both light and salt. Let your light shine and be sure that your life gives forth the savor of salt which is good. If you do this, your witness will certainly be blessed: to a few, or possibly to a large number.

I am a woman who works in a laundry. Our work is very hard and uninteresting. All day long there is complaining by those with whom I work. I have been very troubled about this matter lately. Can you help me find an answer to this problem?

If we live for this life alone, then there are no doubt situations and conditions that would cause one to complain. The difference between the genuine Christian and the non-Christian is more noticeable here than in most places because complaining seems to be such an accepted thing. For the believer in Christ, and for the one who has placed his life in God's hand, there is little cause for complaint. We are told that we are to do our assigned tasks "Not in the way of eye service, as men pleasers: but as servants of Christ, doing the will of God from the heart; with good will doing service as unto the Lord and not unto man" (Ephesians 6:6–7). Faith in God and surrender to Christ involve the whole of life. Your life is planned, and your complaint is against His plan. If "All things work together for good to them that love God, even to those who are called according to His purpose," then you will glorify God by your present disposition. Pity those who complain, and try to use their complaint as an opportunity to present God's plan for their lives as the solution.

I am a Christian businessman, but somehow I never prosper as many others do who are not Christians. In fact, God seems to overlook their wickedness and prosper them. This troubles me, though I don't intend to forsake my faith because of it. Is there any explanation that will put my mind at rest in the matter?

There have been others who have had the same dilemma. One who spoke with authority, David the Psalmist, was confronted with the problem and it troubled him for a long time. Not until he got a vision of the final judgment did he see the issue. What you are doing is looking at the matter without any perspective.

When David finally got the right point of view, he wrote it down for our help and said: "Behold, these are the ungodly who prosper in the world, they increase in riches. Verily I have cleansed my heart in vain." In other words, he felt for a moment that righteousness did not pay. Then he said, "When I thought to know this it was too painful for me, until I went into the Sanctuary of God, then understood I their end" (Psalm 73:12–13, 16, 17).

You must never look upon the immediate profits of any action, but upon their outcome in the final judgment.

Since becoming a Christian I have the problem of being in business with a man who is not one, and who does not conduct the business on Christian principles. My life's investment is in the business, so I can't very well leave without tremendous loss. What shall I do to make him change?

Your problem is a complex one for it also involves the matter of your Christian stewardship. You want to live your life and conduct your affairs as a Christian, and at the same time you must be custodian of your earnings and regard them as a stewardship. Many prosperous men make the mistake that is warned against in the Bible saying: "My power and the might of my hand hath gotten me this wealth." We have the right to say only that it is the Lord who "giveth thee power to get wealth" (Deuteronomy 8:17).

But your partner has a conscience even if he is not a Christian. He will recognize the merit and rightness of the "Christian way" even though he may not accept the redemption provided in Christ for sinners. Get him to conduct the business on Christian principles as a trial and then depend upon God to change his heart.

I work in one of the shops in our city among some very ungodly men. Our work is done on a quota basis, and over the established quota we receive a bonus. The men are not producing a fraction of what they could, but they still insist that we chisel on time so the bonus will be easy to get. My conscience bothers me so much that I feel that I must report this matter to the authorities. Would I be wrong in doing so?

I believe that every employee should be an honest worker, earning his total wage. I also believe that the employer should deal honestly with his workers and give them the full reward for their efforts. I do not see how you can cover the dishonest practice of your group when you know what they are doing and when you approve their actions by doing so yourself. Most of the troubles, if not all, that go on between labor and management would cease if both would adopt such a policy. It is not likely that either of them will do so unless there is a beginning somewhere. Perhaps you are to be the one who acts according to the highest ethics, and in so doing you may influence your entire working situation. The men with whom you work do not need to know how the employer received knowledge of their dishonesty. He will carefully manage such situations. If he does not, you had better find your employment elsewhere. A basic principle of Christianity is fair play and fair work. Non-Christians will be deeply affected by such courage and forthrightness.

My husband and I want to teach our children the dangers of drinking alcohol but we are invited to parties where, for business reasons, we may find it necessary to take a sip or two so as not to hurt the feelings of our hostess. What shall we do?

Why ask me? By your own admission you consider the feelings of your hostess more important than setting an example for your children. Never forget this: you cannot fool your children with pious phrases if they see inconsistencies in your life. There are many people in the world who, "for business reasons," have compromised their convictions. Such compromises hurt the individual and they hurt those they love. Years ago a man left his home, walking in the snow, to go to a place of ill repute. As he left this place he met his son, taking giant strides through the snow. When asked what he was doing, the little fellow said, "I am walking in your steps, Daddy." If you want your children to grow up to be good men and women, surely you must set them such an example in your own home.

I am associated with a man in business who is active in his church on Sunday but who cheats his customers during the week. This has disgusted me with Christianity.

Some of your customers may possibly pay you with a ten-dollar bill which proves to be a counterfeit. Will you stop accepting ten-dollar bills because of a counterfeit? If your business associate is a hypocrite, it is he who is wrong, not Christianity. One can but wonder how you are working out the proceeds of the cheating you mention. If you are profiting by it, you are just as guilty as he. To be perfectly frank, one can but wonder if your so-called disgust with Christianity is not really an excuse for not being a Christian. You know that all of us need Christ. He alone can change our hearts and give us the grace and strength to live as a Christian should live. You evidently have high ideals for Christians. That is fine. See that you live up to those ideals in your own life. Let me urge you to give your heart to Christ so that you can set the right example before Him. If you do this, both of you will honor the name of the Christ you profess.

Chapter 8

How to Be Happy Most of the Time

I am the mother of one illegitimate child and am expecting the second one. Recently I was converted. Where can I begin the new life and how can I leave the old life behind with two children born in sin?

When a group of Pharisees brought a woman to Jesus who had been taken in the act of adultery, Jesus asked them to cast a stone at her, whoever was without sin (John 8:1–11). When it appeared that there was no sinless one to cast the first stone, they departed. Then Jesus said to the woman, "Neither do I condemn thee, go and sin no more." Repentance and faith are genuine and valid when the sinner enters a new way of life. There may be the reminders of the past with you, but you can have this assurance that there is no sin that cannot be forgiven to those who desire the new life that comes about through our faith in Jesus Christ. Begin by being the mother you should be, praying for your children and bringing them up in the knowledge of Christ. The time will come when they will recognize the transformation wrought in your life.

I cannot forget the abortion that was performed on me. Can you help me find peace of mind?

You did not give any details about your case. You must know that legitimate abortions are performed every day by

95

doctors who sometimes have to take this course to save the mother and the home.

Assuming that the termination of your pregnancy was for selfish reasons, it is clear that you have sinned, as did the parties who had a part in it. God gives life, and we have no right to take it. But we are not to assume that this sin is unforgivable. Moses once killed a man, but found forgiveness, and went on to become one of history's great emancipators. Saul of Tarsus had participated in the execution of Stephan, but he had an encounter with Christ on the Damascus Road, and became the first and perhaps greatest Christian missionary. To despair over the magnitude of your sin will only make matters worse. My suggestion is that you come to Him Who said: "Come unto Me all ye that labor and are heavy laden, and I will give you rest." No person, regardless of the extent of his sin, ever responded to this call without finding rest of soul. Don't you delay any longer. God is ready, able, and willing to forgive you and give you His peace.

I have been a loyal church member for many years, but I have never experienced the kind of peace that you are always preaching about. How can I get this peace? Should I leave my church and join another one in order to find it, or will God show me the way through prayer?

There is no church that can give you peace, otherwise more than sixty per cent of the people of the United States would have peace because more than fifty per cent of them are affiliated with churches. It should be obvious, then, that church and religious affiliation can never guarantee peace. It may, however, act as a sedative and provide a temporary satisfaction. This would only deceive you. Peace with God comes through a personal relationship with Him. It is the kind of peace that was made possible by the sacrifice of Christ. The Bible says: "For He is our peace, who made both one, and broke down the middle wall of partition; having abolished in His flesh the enmity, even the law of commandments contained in ordinances; that He might create in Himself of the two one new man, so making peace, and might reconcile them both in one body unto God through the cross, having slain the enmity thereby. And He came and preached peace to you that were far off, and peace to them that were nigh" (Ephesians 2:14–17). This is the kind of peace that you need and you can only find it through that personal act of faith in Christ.

I am discouraged and afraid. My religion has failed me, and now I wonder if a change would bring new hope to me. Would you recommend that I make such a change?

Your plight reminds me of a man I know who had an outdated car which gave him a lot of trouble. He took it to several mechanics who tried to tune it up, but the old motor continued to start hard, miss and jerk. One day a smart mechanic talked him into installing a new motor, and that was the end of his trouble.

For you to just "change your religion" would be like taking the old motor to a new garage. Nothing is more frustrating than trying to be religious without the "new life" that comes when we are born anew. It is like trying to start an old car by pushing it uphill.

So my suggestion to you is: let Christ change your life so that your religion becomes something spontaneous and joyous. Confess your sin, your failures, and your doubts, and say: "Christ, from this moment on, You are in charge of my life." Just stop trying and trust, and you will be amazed at what will happen if you turn all the keys of your life over to Him. Repent of your sins and receive Christ by faith. This is conversion—and you need to be converted!

I'm very mixed up in my spiritual life. At times, I think I'm a Christian and enjoy all the things that Christians enjoy. Then I suddenly have a strong yearning to return to the old life of sin. I know I wouldn't be happy if I did return, but the fact that I sometimes feel like I want to bothers me. How can you explain such a thing?

Your problem is not too unusual although most people don't like to admit it. It is the age-old problem of the spiritual conflict that goes on within each of us. It may be an aggravated condition with you which makes it so serious.

Paul once wrote: "For the flesh lusteth against the Spirit and the Spirit against the flesh; for these are contrary the one to the other; that ye may not do the things that ye would" (Galatians 5:17). This is the battle or the tension that is present in us to a greater or lesser degree. So you see, the spiritual lag that you feel is explained in the Bible.

That does not mean that you accept it as the way it should be. You should make all necessary preparation for this battle which the Bible says "is not against flesh and blood, but against spiritual forces." In Ephesians, chapter six, the Bible tells what preparation you should make. In the meantime, always remember that "Where sin abounds Grace did much more abound" (Romans 5:20).

You can have complete victory! We are told to submit ourselves unto God and the devil will flee from us. We are also promised that "Sin shall not reign over us."

I have always respected my father until a few weeks ago when I discovered that he had a prison record. Now I wonder if I shouldn't leave home and try to forget him?

You react to this discovery of yours just like so many people do. Of course a prison record is not a thing to be desired. But there must have been something fine about your father to call for your respect up until this time. Don't you realize that a change has taken place to make him a respectable citizen and a father you have been able to love? I do not believe that you should leave home for such a reason, nor should you hold it against your father. Be grateful that he did not continue in a life of crime, and encourage him by giving him your complete confidence. Remember that God has granted His forgiveness to us for the taking. He does not hold against us the past when we receive His Son as our Saviour. He freely forgives and forgets for the sake of His Son. It is this forgiveness and confidence that He shows us that provides the incentive to righteous living.

I have just completed a prison sentence of three years. Upon returning to my home, I find that I am not accepted in society any more. I have no work, and almost no friends. Do you think that I am wrong in being so resentful toward people who will have little to do with me? I want to go straight, but it seems that people want to push me back down where I was.

It is one of the problems common to every person who has violated the law and been imprisoned. Your problem is not new. What you must realize is that you have given them a reason for distrusting you, and now it is up to you to give society a reason for accepting you. It won't be easy, and it is one of the aspects of your punishment. I would suggest two things for you to do. First, face the fact that the burden is upon you to convince society of your purpose to go straight. This will take time and will be painful for you, but it will be worth the effort. Second, discover a power that will hold you true to the purpose you have set before you. You cannot go the road alone, for you too are a social creature. Remember that to begin with, God made you to have fellowship. Even though society cannot forget quickly your crime, God will forgive your sins the moment you take Jesus Christ as your Saviour. You have already gone halfway in repentance in being sorry for your sin. Why not go the other half of the way and turn to God who right now is seeking for your heart and for your faith? If you do that, He will sustain you through the days of readjustment, and even more, He will keep you to the end of life in fellowship that is more precious than the best friend can provide.

Some time ago I recognized my sinfulness and began going to church. For a time I felt better but I was not able to overcome the habits that troubled me. Must I always go on with this unrest in my mind? Is there a solution?

It is quite possible by church attendance and other religious exercises to quiet our conscience temporarily. We may even be helped considerably and our moral standards may be definitely raised, but this is not enough! For Jesus said: "Except a man be born again he cannot see the Kingdom of Heaven." A spiritual regeneration is an absolute necessity according to the words of Jesus. Do not let religion take the place of the new birth. Rather, I would urge you to make a decision to receive Christ into your life and experience the new birth. This way you will obtain a real victory. Then even the church will mean more to you.

I would advise you getting alone with your Bible—read Romans 10:9—quietly confess Christ. When you have had this encounter with the living Christ, your whole life will be changed.

A few months ago I think I became a Christian. I'm not really sure though, because the decision didn't solve any of my problems. In fact, I have had more trouble since then. Isn't Christianity supposed to solve problems for you?

Yes, a personal faith does solve problems for you, but it doesn't solve them in exactly the way you think they should be solved. You see, a vital faith doesn't take you out of the world, it doesn't pay your bills, it doesn't cure every sickness. You will still have those problems. Paul the Apostle had a serious problem, and he prayed about it very earnestly. The problem remained, but God gave Paul enough strength to live with the problem, and that may be what you are supposed to do. The Lord said: "My grace is sufficient for thee, for my strength is made perfect in weakness" (II Corinthians 12:9).

A true faith in Jesus Christ completely solves a certain class of problems, principally that of sin. This is really man's greatest problem, and from sin come all of the other problems. Salvation is not like aspirin, dulling the nerves to feeling. Salvation goes to the root of the problem and makes a new person out of you. "Him who knew no sin, He made to be sin on our behalf, that we might become the righteousness of God in Him" (II Corinthians 5:21).

My mother committed suicide some time ago. I have since then been obsessed with the fear that I would do the same

*thing sometime. Can you tell me how to overcome such a
fear?*

Apart from any religious meaning, I believe you are suffering
from a kind of identification with your mother, which is a
common thing. No doubt you cared for your mother and
also believe that you might have some of the same potential
within yourself. You must recognize the fact that there is
no reason why you should be compelled to do the same, unless it is a result of concentrating on it. You must divert your
mind and begin to think on something else.

Your problem is not only psychological but also spiritual.
If you have given yourself completely to Christ and are absolutely surrendered to His control, there can be no thought
of suicide. The Apostle Paul once said: "Don't worry over
anything whatever. Tell God every detail of your needs in
earnest and thankful prayer, and the peace of God which
transcends human understanding will keep your hearts and
minds as they rest in Christ Jesus." The Apostle again said:
"Fix your minds on the things which are right and pure and
beautiful and good." Christ can so completely change your
nature and control your mind that you can find complete relief and joy in serving Him. I would suggest that you see
your minister and have a frank discussion with him.

*I thought that when I became a Christian my problems would
somehow be solved. I have had almost more since I became
a Christian. What should we expect when we receive Christ?*

You should not expect the easy way, for if you do you are
certainly destined for disappointment. Any person who knows
the Bible knows that the Christian life is likened to an
athletic contest or to warfare, and neither one is easy. Jesus
said: "In the world ye shall have tribulation, but be of good
cheer, I have overcome the world." In the Bible it is said of
Satan that he "Goeth about as a roaring lion seeking whom
he may devour," and that certainly does not speak of an
easy way. Jesus warned His followers to count carefully the
cost.

But there is no good thing that comes without cost. The Christian life is most satisfying, but only when we actually go all out and all the way. It is the Christian who tries to compromise who finds life miserable, for he has all the problems without the fellowship that comes through surrender. For every trial and test, Christ supplies an abundance of grace with which to bear it, and in our weakness we are made strong (II Corinthians 12:10).

I have been told that there is no happiness without being a Christian. As a young person, I am finding my happiness in wonderful friends, amusements, and in wholesome activity. I sometimes think I should be a Christian and go to church, but many of the folks I find there are not as happy as I am. Their religion makes them sad and without the fun of life. Is this a part of the Christian life?

True Christianity is seldom found in any one person or even in a group. If certain qualities are present, frequently others are absent. There are many who actually believe that joy and happiness are worldly, while others seek only for the good time. The Christian life is the only genuinely happy life for the happiness and joy of the Christian does not depend upon circumstances. You said that you found yours all in such things as friends, amusements and wholesome recreation. But soon these will fail to provide your joy. Any happiness based on circumstances can quickly change. Only when our joy is founded upon an unchanging person and upon an unfailing love can it endure. Certainly you are not so foolish as to think that your joy will last. Seek the joy that comes from surrender to Christ, and you will have something that will abide through changing conditions and circumstances.

I grew up in a Christian home, but a few years ago I began chasing around with the gang, and did things I'm ashamed of. Now I've met a wonderful girl, and want to be decent. How can I get rid of the ugly memories that torment me?

Truly repent. Get down on your knees and ask God to forgive you. Of course you don't deserve it, but God loves you. He sent His Son to wash away your sins. Accept Jesus as your Saviour. Follow Christ. Let Him lead you into a new life. When you've made a fresh, clean start, God will wipe away all record of your sins. He will remember them no more. You must do the same. Forget the past, except to profit by it. Press on to the future, always asking Christ what you should do.

Say, as Paul did: "This one thing I do, forgetting those things which are behind, and reaching forth unto those things which are before, I press toward the mark for the prize of the high calling of God in Christ Jesus" (Philippians 3:13–14). The high calling Paul is speaking of is service. Think not of yourself, but of others. Have you harmed anyone? Then make restitution just as soon as you can. If this is not possible, plan to add to the security and happiness of someone else.

I can hear you say, "Billy, nothing I can ever do will right the wrong I've done." Well, do the best you can. Then give thanks for Christ. He alone can save you! Accept Him at His word, surrender your life to Him, and you will find peace.

Chapter 9

The Best Way to Resist Temptation

I am a Christian, I believe, but am always faced with strong temptation. Is there any way to overcome such temptation?

God never promised to remove temptation from us, for even Christ was subject to it. The Bible says that "He was tested in all things like as we, yet without sin." There is really no good reason why you should seek to escape, for such times of testing have beneficial effects. "Tribulation worketh patience and patience experience and experience hope, and hope maketh not ashamed." There is a sense of achievement and assurance that results from victory over temptation that cannot come to us otherwise. Temptation really shows what people really are. It does not make us Christian or un-Christian. It does make the Christian stronger and causes him to discover resources of power. It also makes evident that false profession and hypocrisy of the non-Christian. You can benefit from what might be tragedy if you will only discover that in just such a time of temptation, Christ can become more real to you than ever, and His salvation will become more meaningful.

I want to do right but I am too weak to overcome temptation. What hope is there for me?

You are exactly where all of the rest of us are. None of us is strong enough to overcome temptations, regardless of how good our motives may be. That is the reason God sent His Son into the world—to take away the guilt and penalty of our sins and to give us the strength to overcome temptation. May I suggest that your trouble is probably too much looking inside at self and not enough looking outward and upward to Christ who wants to help you. The Bible says: "There hath no temptation taken you but such as is common to man; but God is faithful, who will not suffer you to be tempted above that ye are able; but will with the temptation also make a way of escape, that ye may be able to bear it." When temptations come let me suggest that you ask God for strength and also to show you the way He has prepared for your escape. One other word of counsel: be very sure that you do not deliberately place yourself in a position to be tempted. All of us are not subjected to the same weaknesses and temptations. To one, alcohol may be the temptation; to another it may be impure thoughts and acts; to another greed and covetousness; to another criticism and an unloving attitude. Regardless of what it may be, be sure that Satan will tempt you at your weak point, not the strong. Our Lord has given us an example of how to overcome the devil's temptations. When He was tempted in the wilderness He defeated Satan every time by the use of the Bible. The Psalmist tells us how to do this when he says: "Thy word have I hid in mine heart, that I might not sin against Thee."

I am a Christian and read my Bible and pray. Just recently I have begun to have very evil and wicked thoughts. I can't stop them from entering my mind. What can I do?

Your experience is not surprising, nor abnormal. It is Satan's purpose to steal the seed of truth from your heart by sending distracting thoughts. It should encourage you to know that the devil considers you a good enough Christian to use as a target.

The difference between a Christian and a non-Christian is: though they both may have good and evil thoughts, Christ gives His followers strength to select the right rather than the wrong. You see a man going to prayer meeting with a Bible under his arm. That man was undoubtedly tempted to stay at home, go bowling, or to some other activity. But, as these diverse thoughts came to his mind, he made the right selection, and headed for the church. Another man walks through the night to a bar. It no doubt occurred to him that he had best stay home with his family. But, he yielded to a negative thought, and gave in to his lower appetites.

It is not the thoughts you have, but the decision you make about them that counts. "He will not suffer us to be tempted above that we are able to bear," says the Bible.

The little girl said, "When the devil knocks at my door I just send Jesus to the door."

For many years I lived a very wicked life. Since I decided for Christ last summer things have been different. But I still can't get over the craving for alcohol. Can you help me?

The same Lord who changed the direction of your life last summer can give you victory over this terrible appetite. But I would caution you first: don't think that the temptation means you are not truly converted. Such a habit has its physical as well as its spiritual effects. Alcoholism is a kind of illness, but it was caused by your sinful desires. Now you must rely upon Christ to give you more power than the power of the habit. You are feeling the effects of the years of sin that preceded your decision.

Second, I would urge you to give your attention to the spiritual food you need. You can get this only through a systematic study of the Bible. Sermons will help, but they do not take the place of personal study of God's Word. Peter said, "As newborn babes, desire the sincere milk of the word that ye may grow thereby" (I Peter 2:2).

Third, pray frequently. When the tempter comes, go to God in prayer. While you are in prayer, the devil has no power, but he will flee from you. Tell God all about your trouble and ask Him for deliverance.

Some time ago I read one of your answers concerning evil thoughts. I, too, am troubled with evil thoughts that are actually blasphemous. I am greatly troubled over this because the more I try to dismiss them from my mind, the more they trouble me. In fact, the problem grows worse as I try to overcome it. I am a Christian and wish to please God. Is there any answer to this problem?

It is known that we cannot always control the thoughts we have. In fact, you will find that your desperate attempt to dismiss them from your mind is exactly the thing that keeps them active. It is just like most spiritual struggles. They are not overcome by our own self will and determination. The best resolution will not overcome the enemy. Only when we admit our helplessness, and call upon God to deliver us, will we find deliverance. As long as you try by your own strength, you will fail, but when you draw upon the resources of His strength, you will find relief.

You are worried about the wickedness of these thoughts. As long as you disapprove them, you are well, but when the time comes that you approve them and affirm them with your will, then you are certainly in a low spiritual condition. Paul once said: "Finally, brethren, whatsoever things are true, whatsoever things are honorable, whatsoever things are just, whatsoever things are pure, whatsoever things are lovely, whatsoever things are of good report, if there be any virtue, if there be any praise, think on these things."

I ride in a car pool of which my boss is also a member. On an increasing number of occasions he has made improper advances to me but has never done so in the office. If I am not careful I may lose my job. What should a Christian do?

A Christian should also be a lady, and you should insist that you be treated as such. It is my opinion that you will not lose your job if you insist that your boss respect you. But, it would be far better to lose your position than to submit to something which is suggestive or degrading. Our moral standards have slipped so much that many people take laxness of behavior as a matter of course. There is nothing more needed than for Christian people to raise up the standard of purity and moral principles which are a vital part of

the Christian faith. Fear of losing a job has been the downfall of more than one person. Others have faced the issue
and in most cases they are respected for their stand. I know
of a young woman who rejected the advances of a man and
who in so doing led him to Christ. Men may try to take advantage of you but you earn their respect by standing for
those principles the Bible so clearly affirms and which you
in your own heart know to be right.

Chapter 10

Antidote for Loneliness and Failure

I have been falsely accused of a dishonest act. Everyone seems to think that I am guilty, but before God, I am innocent. What can I do when all are against me in this matter?

Men usually judge by appearances, and from their opinions of us in this way. Perhaps they did not even see you in a place where such a thing could be done. Nevertheless you are guilty in their opinion, and they may not change quickly.

The first thing to do is to make sure that you are not only without blame in the matter, but that you give no reason for their suspicions. You are being closely watched so that the opinions of men can be confirmed, if possible.

There is something more important. We must all finally give an answer to God only for our every act. You may have to bear the stigma of the rumor for many years. If it is without any foundation in fact, your conscience can be clear. There are many who would give their last dollar for a clear conscience. Thank God for that blessing. Thank God also that you are not afraid to stand in His presence, for if you have placed your trust in Christ, you have nothing to fear for eternity. You can depend on the Scripture that tells us that "Man looketh upon the outward appearance, but God looketh upon the heart."

There is a verse in the Bible that says "Whatsoever is born of God doth not commit sin." I used to think of myself as a

Christian, but I know that I have sinned. Does that mean that I am not a child of God?

I think that you are referring to the Scripture found in I John 3:9. Many people are confused by this verse. What it actually means is that whoever is begotten of God does not sin as a way of life or he does not continually practice sin. Don't let your failures or your weaknesses discourage you. If in your heart you desire to live in fellowship with God, and if you have confessed Christ as your Saviour, you have the assurance that His blood does cleanse all sin.

The verse should be translated thus: "Whosoever is born of God doth not practice sin."

I feel frustrated because of my inability to make satisfactory adjustments to my business associates. I think I have tried the usual methods to make adjustments, but wondered if there might be some therapy in religion that would put me on the road to a more satisfactory adjustment?

Multitudes of people are frustrated in this day of extreme tension and keen competition. But to think of religion as being nothing more than a therapy is to have an inadequate concept of it. The true Christian faith is a new life, not merely making adjustment of the old life.

There are certain religious attitudes that may provide temporary relief. The Christian faith is more than a means to an end, it is the end itself. It is a complete release from all of the old life and a discovery of a life that possesses an entirely new dimension. Yes, I can give you an answer to your problem, but unless you are ready to abandon your old life in favor of the new, you are just deceiving yourself. The new life Paul describes saying: "The life that I now live in the flesh, I live by the faith of the Son of God who loved me and gave Himself for me." This must begin by being "converted." This means "repenting" of sin and "receiving" Christ into your life. When this is done, a change takes place. You will find a new and dynamic power to help you live the Christian life.

I am a young man with average talents and, I believe, acceptable appearance and manners. I never seem to be able to make friends, because sooner or later those who seem to be friends all leave me. I need friends just as much as anyone does. Is there some hidden secret to this business of making and keeping friends?

No, there is no hidden secret in the matter of making and keeping friends. You make one statement in your letter that indicates why you cannot keep friends. You are selfish, and want friends for your own satisfaction. To have friends, you must first be friendly. You must offer your unselfish friendship to another and expect nothing in exchange. The deepest joy of abiding friendship is to have one upon whom you can lavish your friendship without demanding anything for yourself. This may sound strange to you, but it is the foolproof way to get a friend. The Bible offers the world's best example. It says of God that "We love Him because He first loved us." This is the completely unselfish love that sent Christ to Calvary and made atonement for our sins. You may think your problem has no religious implications, but it does. Man, left without God, is basically selfish. In conversion, this selfishness is exchanged for a selflessness. Christians find their joy in giving themselves even as Christ gave Himself, and they are never without the joy and satisfaction of friends.

I am a Christian girl, and am considered to be reasonably attractive. But I'm disappointed in that fellows just don't go for me. I'm like any girl, and would like to date. Is it possible for a girl to be too strait-laced for even nice boys?

No, not for the kind of boy you deserve. Remember that many dates are brought about by physical desire, and only incidentally because of genuine appreciation of the finer qualities one may possess. As one who is dedicated to Christ, you want more than a boy who is drawn to you physically.

As a Christian, you must believe that God has a plan for your life. Just as He has for every life. God once said to an ancient king, "I have surnamed thee though thou has not known me" (Isaiah 45:4). Much more then, God has a plan for your life, seeing that you have given it to Him.

What it means is that somewhere there is God's choice of a young man for you, and you would never be happy with any other. Rather than to spend your energy being concerned over your problem, commit it to the Lord, and He will direct in this as in every other matter of life.

I married a man who claims he is a blue blood, and he has a superior attitude toward people who are not what he calls "blooded stock." At times he makes me feel very inferior because my folks came from the wrong side of the tracks. Can you help me?

If your husband wanted to retain pedigreed stock, why did he marry you, a commoner?

When a member of a prominent New England family boasted to Will Rogers that her ancestors came over on the *Mayflower,* the humorist, who was proud of his Indian blood, said, "My ancestors were here to meet them."

A great American who, according to your husband, was born on the "wrong side of the tracks" once said: "Our fathers brought forth on this continent a new nation . . . dedicated to the proposition that all men are created equal."

But Lincoln's words were a reflection of the Christian ethic which says: "For there is no difference . . . he is a Jew who is one inwardly . . . in the spirit, and not in the letter; whose praise is not of men, but of God."

Sin cannot be bred out of men, and goodness cannot be bred into them, "For all have sinned and come short of the glory of God." All men stand in need of God's grace if they are to be the ladies and gentlemen they ought to be.

Both my brother and sister are very brilliant. I am just ordinary. They get many chances to do work in our church while I only get a few. This makes me feel very discouraged,

*for I feel the Lord can't use me like He does them. How can
I avoid getting so discouraged?*

No Christian, old or young, needs to be discouraged over
such things. In the world there is stiff competition but in
God's work there is none. The Bible plainly teaches that "To
whomsoever much is given, much shall be required: and to
whom they commit much of him will they ask the more"
(Luke 12:48). What God expects, and all God expects, is
that we dedicate completely all of our talents and gifts to
Him. That is the meaning of the parable of the talents in
Matthew 25. Read this parable, and you will see that we
are always rewarded because of our faithfulness. You can
be just as faithful as anyone and have the commendation of
the Lord. Take the one talent you have, and invest it in
eternal things. Some talented people lose their reward because they do things to be seen of men. Some untalented
people lose their reward because they fail to dedicate what
they have because it is not noticed by men. Both have sinned
equally.

*I've been in an accident and have an ugly scar on my face.
I fear it will never go away. Do you think I should force
myself to go out and meet people, even though I dread it?*

Of course you should. Your life will be narrow and selfish
if you shut out the world and think only of your own mis-
fortune.

Your real problem is how to conquer your dread of people. The Bible says: "Fear not, for I am thy shield" (Genesis
15:1). As you go out the door of your home think of God
as going before you, opening the eyes of all so they will see
your heart and not your face. The real you can be beautiful,
more lovely than ever before. Your suffering should have
made you more sympathetic and understanding. It will not
be hard for you to meet people if you think of them instead
of yourself. Almost everyone has some trouble. Be eager to
listen, to give your sympathy, and to say words of encouragement. Very few have no handicap. Accept yours, and ask

God to help you forget yourself while you bring joy and comfort to others.

Since I came to Chicago I've been terribly lonely. My neighbors never speak to me. How can people in a Christian country be so cruel?

Have you ever thought that some of your neighbors may feel lonesome, too? You don't need to wait for them to speak first. Reach over the back fence and share something from your garden, or knock on the door of the next apartment and bring a bit of something you have been baking. On every side are people who will welcome a smile, and a friendly word.

Go to church on Sunday, and when the service is over don't hurry away. In the churches of Chicago, as in every town and city, there are warmhearted people who are eager to welcome a stranger into the Christian fellowship. You must do your part by giving them an opportunity.

There are thousands like you in every big city. But you don't need to be lonely. Christ is your friend, closer to you than a brother. Surrender your heart to Him, and you'll find He is with you wherever you are. He said: "I will never leave thee, nor forsake thee" (Hebrews 13:5). This is our Master's promise, and we can trust His word. With Jesus beside you, and Christian friends to support you, you can feel at home anywhere.

I should have graduated last June, but failed in my examinations. Now I can't get a decent job, and feel I'll never make good. Can you help me?

It isn't easy to be left behind, but it's never too late to make a fresh start. If you failed because you didn't do your best each day, this should be a lesson to you. You can't waste time today, and expect to make it up when the hour of testing comes. This is true in business as well as in school.

Now you can let your failure be an excuse to run away

from life's challenge, or you can profit by it. Through the saving power of Christ you can, if necessary, live a victorious life even while doing dull, uninteresting tasks. The Bible says: "In all these things we are more than conquerors through Him that loved us" (Romans 8:37). We find this is true when we accept from Jesus the help He offers each one of us.

Ask God how He would have you use your life. Our Father has a work for each one of us. Go to your minister, and seek his advice. Then, whether you go back to school or get a job, get down on your knees each morning and pray that God will guide you. We all have resources within us that rarely are tapped. With God's help you'll discover hidden strength, and be able to accomplish many things you never could do alone.

Chapter 11

How to Cure a Bad Habit

I have no patience with people who get intoxicated, but do you think a little social drinking to promote good fellowship does any harm?

Of course it does. Can you be blind to the fact that one drink often leads to another? In every city I visit someone asks me to pray for a husband, or wife, or son who started as a social drinker and now has become an alcoholic. Today you think you have perfect self-control. But if you make a habit of drinking what will you do when you face anxiety or disappointment?

You also have some responsibility for the welfare of your neighbor. Your example may lead him into a habit he cannot break. If you encourage him to do anything which brings his downfall, you are guilty. And don't forget that alcohol is the cause of many of our traffic accidents, and a man who commits murder on the highway because his responses are slow, or he doesn't see where he's going, is guilty in the sight of God.

Our bodies are the temples of our souls. We must treat them with respect. The Bible says: "Whether therefore ye eat, or drink, or whatsoever ye do, do all to the glory of God" (I Corinthians 10:31). This is a command no Christian should ignore.

Is there any help or hope for an alcoholic? I am one and have a very guilty feeling about it. It preys on my mind constantly even when I am asleep. Everyone tells me I must give up drinking, but it isn't that easy. I cannot destroy the craving that I have for liquor, yet in my mind I want to be rid of it. I feel depressed and resentful, and it is so bad that every night when I go to bed I hope I will never awaken again.

Yes, there definitely is hope for an alcoholic. Many alcoholics have been converted to Jesus Christ and have been completely delivered from the terrible craving that they have had for many years.

Although there are many organizations that do provide excellent help for the alcoholic, yet Jesus Christ can provide the greatest therapy for the disease.

Those who know something about alcoholism tell us that the first step toward deliverance is to have a strong desire for deliverance and to admit the fact, "I am alcoholic." In saying this, they have stated a tremendous truth, for you can never be saved from your sins until you first of all admit, "I am a sinner," and then have a desire to have your life changed.

Jesus Christ can change your life. He said: "I am come that ye might have life, and that ye might have it more abundantly." Drunkenness is a sin according to the Bible and must be treated that way, although it develops into a sickness. Thus to go at the heart of the matter and treat it as sin—finding God's forgiveness—often provides a "cure." I know many who would gladly testify to this "miracle" in their lives.

Why do some Christians speak out against such habits as smoking, et cetera, and you seem to say little or nothing about them? Isn't it time to make known the evils of such practices?

The medical profession has done an excellent job in alerting the American public to the dangers of smoking. A multitude of magazine articles and medical reports has established the relationship of the habit with the occurrence of lung cancer. But God did not call me to militate against any particular vice, but to proclaim Christ. If I were to begin championing causes of one sort or another, it would be difficult to know which particular cause is most worthy.

There is a good reason why so many Christians do speak out against the use of tobacco. The Bible teaches that when a man is converted to Christ and receives pardon for his sin that Christ enters into his heart to dwell. In this sense Christianity is much more than theory or religion. It is a relatedness to Christ. Having come to dwell, we are then to regard the human body as sacred. "Your body is a temple of the Holy Spirit which is in you, which ye have from God, and ye are not your own. For ye were bought with a price; glorify God therefore in your body."

This verse applies to many things—for example, overeating or gluttony, or the wrong use of sex, et cetera. Anything that is harmful to the body is not glorifying God.

Is it a sin to gamble for small stakes? In our office we often "flip" for drinks or for lunch.

At the risk of being called a prude, I must be frank in answering your question about petty gambling.

Most professional gamblers began their careers as petty gamblers, just as most alcoholics began their drinking moderately. There is something alluring about getting something for nothing, I realize that. And that is where the sin of it lies. Gambling of any kind amounts to "theft" by permission. The coin is flipped, the dice are rolled, or the horses run, and somebody rakes in that which belongs to another. The Bible says: "In the sweat of thy face shalt thou eat bread." It doesn't say, "By the flip of a coin, shalt thou eat thy lunch." I realize that in most petty gambling no harm is intended. But the principle is the same as in big gambling. The difference is only in the amount of money involved.

Gambling in the United States in a recent year amounted to $21,000,000,000; while the cost of all crime was $20,000,-000,000. More than twice as much is spent for gambling as is spent on alcohol and milk and dairy products. It is the principal folly of man. And one of the sad things about it is that most of the profits go to the big syndicates who are out to beat the small gambler.

I have difficulty sleeping at night without sleeping tablets. Is it wrong to use artificial aids for sleep?

Physicians say that five millions in America must take sleeping tablets in order to sleep. I heard of one man who set his alarm clock for 2 A.M. to wake himself up, so he could take another pill.

Lack of sleep is caused by a number of things: tension, worry, and the lack of proper work or exercise. The Bible suggests another reason for sleeplessness: "The wicked are like the troubled sea, when it cannot rest, whose waters cast up mire and dirt" (Isaiah 57:20). Though I would not say that believing Christians are never troubled with insomnia, I do believe that much sleeplessness is caused by a troubled conscience. I used to have sleepless nights when thoughts of my critics raced through my mind. But as I dropped on my knees and asked God to fill my heart with His love, I have found peace—and rest.

Try repeating this verse from Isaiah over and over in your mind when you can't sleep: "Thou wilt keep him in perfect peace whose mind is stayed on Thee." Let thoughts of God's love, holiness, and majesty fill your mind, and I believe it will help you to find rest and relaxation.

I am addicted to dope and want to break the habit. My parents don't know about it and I don't dare ask them for the money for doctors and hospital to get cured. They would be heartbroken if they knew about it, so what can I do?

Sooner or later every sin brings its own penalty and you are already paying the price for a "fling." No doubt you already see a relationship between your ways and a spiritual problem or you would not have asked us for help. I have this word of encouragement for you, because I have known persons addicted to dope to be delivered from it when they sincerely repented of all their sins and turned to Christ for deliverance. Any medical cure would be nothing more than temporary, for you might be brought under the influence again unless you experience a complete change of heart and life. This is just what Jesus Christ can do for you.

I don't believe you are giving your parents a chance when you refuse to confide in them. If they would be heartbroken because of your condition, they would be more so if they were left to discover it some other way. Go to them with your problem, and if they are what parents should be, they will go to the limit to help you find a way out.

I have an uncontrollable tongue and I know it. It is just my nature to talk, talk, talk; but it bothers my husband, and I would like to overcome it. What would you suggest?

Your desire to stop is the first step, and here are a few suggestions: (1) ask the Lord to give you a love for and a genuine interest in other people; (2) develop the art of being and agreeable companion, you will learn a lot; and (3) if a good listener; not only will you become a more charming you simply have to talk be constructive, kind, humorous, interesting. Whatever you do, be brief. Solomon says, "In the multitude of words there wanteth not sin." It has been wisely said, "To be able to converse in several languages is valuable; to be able to hold your tongue in one is priceless." Remember, the greatest talkers are seldom great conversationalists, and always, great bores.

When traffic brushes occur when I am driving I find myself calling other drivers vile names. They don't hear me. I excuse myself by saying that it is a good psychological safety valve. As a Christian must I overcome such a habit?

In answering let me ask you a question. Why is it that an otherwise decent, law-abiding, God-fearing citizen so often becomes vile, uncouth, and ungentlemanly when he drives an automobile? It makes no moral difference whether or not the other driver heard you, although it might make a physical difference should he hear you—unless you are a good fighter or can run pretty fast. The driver's wheel may change him into something approaching the subhuman, also. Your changed personality behind the wheel tends toward more accidents. Decency and courtesy contribute a great deal to safety on our highways. Indecency and discourtesy not only endanger others but also are denials of anything Christlike. Frankly, I doubt your sincerity in asking the question.

I am an entertainer and work at night. I do feel my need of God, but lately I have taken to drink. I sometimes feel that life is so futile and empty. Is there any help for me?

Yes, of course there is help for you. Offhand I would say you are in a rut, and a rut is nothing but a long, narrow grave. Your life seems futile and empty principally because up to now it *has been* futile and empty.

But you must not let it continue to be that way. You see, you were not made to live without a purpose. The Bible says that we were "created a little lower than the angels." In short, we were made for God's fellowship. Deep inside us is the awareness of this fact. It is written indelibly upon our hearts and our consciences. That is the reason you feel life is empty—because you have not discovered real purpose.

Now, how can you do it? First, bow before God and say something like this: "Christ, I bring my empty life to you. Please fill it with thy love and grace. Forgive me for wasting my time and talents, and help me to make my life count for something from this moment on." Then claim this promise: "Him that cometh unto me I will in no wise cast out." I have known hundreds of people who found peace by just praying a simple prayer from the heart such as this. Try it, and if you really mean it a miracle will happen. Then go out and share your newfound joy.

I was one of the "converts" in the New York Crusade meeting. My life since then has been entirely different, but I'm discouraged because I still can't get over my sharp temper and some of my old ways of doing things. Must I go on living such a defeated kind of living?

No, for God has made provision for a victorious kind of Christian living. It is all taught in the Bible, and for the new Christian it is most important that you become familiar with its teachings. Let me suggest something that will help you.

First, victory in the Christian life is not faultlessness. The impact of sin makes deep impressions upon all of us, and they do not disappear in a moment. You received new directions when you were born again, but now you must grow.

Second, newborn infants need food regularly and in increasing amounts. As a spiritual babe, you need the food of God's Word. We are told to "Desire the sincere milk of the Word that ye may grow thereby" (I Peter 2:2).

Third, we will be happy to send you Bible helps if you write for them to our Minneapolis office.

Be assured that God can give you victory over your temper. The Scripture promises, "Sin shall not have dominion over you." This means that sin shall not rule or dominate you. Claim the victory by faith.

Chapter 12

Bad Health, Bad Luck, and Bad Morals

I have a Mongoloid child and three other normal children. My doctor tells me I should put our afflicted child in a special home so that our other children will have proper care and be released from the stigma. What do you think?

I would not want to be put into the position of going against your doctor's advice, but experience has shown that Mongoloid children, if given proper understanding and much love, can be habilitated into society. These children are very lovable, and certainly are in need of love and understanding. You speak of a "stigma." I don't see that there should be any reproach on your family because of this abnormal child. Some physically normal children have personality defects which are worse in some ways.

The tendency today is to seek the easy, convenient way out of difficult situations. You must remember that you must live with yourself, and if the guilt feelings you experience outweigh the release from caring for this needy child, it would seem to be an unwise move to send him to a special home.

Giving love is more blessed than receiving it, for the Bible says: "It is more blessed to give than to receive," and this abnormal child needs your love as much or more than your other children.

Also, perhaps God sent you this child for a special reason known at the moment only by God. This child may be what Dale Evans has called an "Angel Unaware."

A recent operation has revealed a cancer so far advanced that there is no possible cure. I am a Christian and I do so want to show it during these remaining months.

God is giving you a marvelous opportunity, and I believe you will rise to it. After all, everyone in this world must face the inevitability of death. Only the Christian knows how to live and how to die. You know that for you, as a Christian, death will be but the opening up of something so wonderful that no human eye has ever seen anything like it, no human ear has ever heard such glories, and in fact the human imagination cannot conjure up what it is like. Because you have this thrilling hope in your own heart, tell other people about it and ask God to give you the presence and power to make it real to others. It can well be that your witness for Him will be the means of bringing many others to the same hope. Remember, too, the future you have with Christ is for all eternity. The last two chapters in the Bible tell something of what heaven is like. Christ came into this world to redeem us and to enable us to live for Him. He also came to enable us to die with the assurance in our hearts that we shall be with Him forever.

I am suffering from what my doctor calls hypertension. He has given me drugs to quiet my nerves but when they are taken regularly their effectiveness wears off. Do you think that prayer and religion would help me, and if so, what steps should I take?

If what you are seeking through prayer and faith is some immediate relief from your hypertension, you will probably be disappointed and say that prayer and religion don't work. You see, a quiet, confident faith is the result of a vital relationship with God, and God will not give you the effects of a living relationship to Him while you bypass the matter of sin and salvation. Many persons are trying to use religion and faith as a sedative or stimulant, whichever they need most. What we all need is a saving faith in Christ that comes as a result of a frank facing of the fact of our personal sin and guilt. It would not surprise me if your hypertension is definitely related to your alienation from God. Why don't you begin at the beginning, take Christ as your Saviour and trust God for the rest.

Every time I plan to go to church my wife fakes a sick spell, or at least it seems so to me. She is never the deceptive type and that's why I'm so puzzled. Why should she behave this way, and how can I help her?

Your wife's illness may be the real thing, and it is not necessarily an attempt to deceive you. People who are spiritually concerned will react in strange ways without knowing why they do so. She may be disturbed over her sin and need of God and her resistance may well cause the nervous reaction. If she were naturally given to deception it would be put on, but there is reason to believe this is not so. Contact a minister who can present the message of Christ to her and explain how her opposition to the gospel might be the only possible explanation for her condition. This could awaken her to her spiritual need. This could easily be a symptom of conviction, which is the first step toward a true encounter with Christ. When she finds His forgiveness, I think you will find this strange reaction leaving her.

My husband and I go to church quite regularly. One thing that disturbs me greatly is that he always has to leave the service shortly after the sermon begins. He then waits in the car for me. He says he can't stand the crowd and other things, yet he seems to be a perfectly well and normal individual. How can you explain such behavior?

Your husband could be horribly bored, but I doubt that, because it is possible to endure the most boring talk for a short time, and besides you seem to enjoy it. Most likely he is being pricked by something he hears each week. When a group of people listened to Peter preaching one time the Bible records that they were "all pricked in their hearts" (Acts 2:37). People do not usually know what is troubling them when they hear the Bible preached. They often feel uncomfortable during a service. This is a sign that the Holy Spirit is convicting them. It is well that your husband is responding so well, for too many people are quite indifferent to the preaching of the Bible. Pray for him and patiently encourage him to continue. God will convict him in answer to your prayers and he may yet come to the happy experience of personal faith in Christ. When this happens, he will suddenly respond with enthusiasm to what he hears, just as you are now enjoying the preaching of God's Word.

Why do you so often suggest that religion is a cure-all, when modern psychiatry has done so much for mentally disturbed persons?

Religion is not a cure-all, but the gospel of Christ certainly is the only answer to the sin problem. If the problem is one that is related to sin and its consequences, then Christ is the answer, and not psychiatry. If the disturbance is purely a mental one, then a competent psychiatrist might give satisfactory help. It would call for a psychiatrist with real spiritual insight to be able to tell the difference between the purely mental problem and the spiritual problem. Let it be known that Christianity is not opposed to everything modern but only such claims that are not totally true and that do injustice to the claims of the gospel. I wish every mentally disturbed person might be counseled by one who knows the functioning of the human mind and knows equally well the message of deliverance through Jesus Christ.

Recently my wife began to show considerable mental derangement. Finally she had to be committed to a hospital for mental patients. My real problem is that she was such a fine Christian. How will this affect her personal salvation and her relationship to the Lord?

Mental problems are very often related to physical conditions. Your letter seems to indicate that this is the case, and especially at her age. I believe she will pass through this period in a reasonable length of time. Meanwhile you do not need to be concerned about her relationship to the Lord. If her walk with God was established before the mental problem arose, you can be sure that God fully understands the matter better than we. We do not lose our salvation in the time of our greatest trials, for it is then that it means more to us than ever. Paul once said: "I am persuaded that neither death nor life nor angels nor principalities, not things present nor things to come nor powers nor height nor depth nor any other creature shall be able to separate us from the love of God which is in Christ Jesus our Lord." This can be your present hope for one you love so much.

Recently a counselor told me that I was a mild neurotic. He based it upon the fact that I am perpetually distressed with the feeling of being lost. Sometimes I think this could drive me into insanity. Can you explain this problem or help me?

First, you may be assured that you will not go into insanity. You would have little awareness of going insane if you were in actual danger. People who finally go insane are neither concerned about it nor do they feel that it is even possible.

Second, your counselor was right in terming your condition as one of neurosis. Any feeling of inadequacy or inferiority is a form of neurosis if we are not being very factual about it. On the other hand, your feeling of lostness may well be a very real and factual condition. If in your early childhood you went to Sunday school or church and heard the teaching of the Bible, you may still remember just enough to give you the sense of being forever lost. The answer to your problem is not to deny the fact but to find salvation. God may have implanted this lost feeling in your soul until you turn to Him for forgiveness and deliverance. I am sure that if you do this, God will replace the lost feeling with one of belonging to Him.

I am the mother of a retarded child, victim of brain damage during birth. Sometimes God seems cruel and heartless to me for a fleeting moment, but I really know that God is just and that all our children will someday be taken to His bosom again.

There are 120,000 retarded children born in America every year. More than four million people are affected by this problem. So you are not alone.

I can sympathize with you, although I have never experienced your particular problem. I realize the heavy burden you are carrying, and it is not lessened by the curiosity of people who leer at the less fortunate, and often blame the parents for any abnormality of a child. These people lack a proper understanding and love.

We cannot blame God for every so-called accident of nature. That would embitter our own lives, and make our sorrow more acute. May I remind you that no life, no situation, no home is perfect. While your problem may be more conspicuous than others, most people have their quota of sorrow and disappointment. They may seem to have escaped difficulties, but if you could see behind the scenes, you would know that they too have heavy burdens.

An implicit faith in God will give you courage, hope, and the ability to accept your lot in life. The Bible says: "Casting all your care on Him, for He careth for you."

I worry constantly. At the present time I am almost on the point of a breakdown. I know this is not fitting for a Christian. All those that I have counseled with tell me there is nothing to worry about, but I know there is much to worry about. With a sick husband, a boy in the Army, an uncertain job, and a few other things, I can't help it. Do you have any suggestions?

For anyone to say you have nothing to worry about is simply showing their ignorance. You certainly have much to worry about. Your problems are great and without God's help, you cannot bear them. You are entitled to worry unless you believe God. Faith and worry are mutually exclusive. I would not tell you that there is nothing to worry about.

But what I would tell you is that there is someone who loves you and cares for you. There is someone who knows your problem, and still better, He can take your cares. The Bible says: "Casting all your care on Him for He careth for you." So, although you have much to worry about, let Jesus take that worry. If He can carry the load of your sin and the sin of the world, He can also bear your present burden, lift the load, and give you inner resources that will enable you to live victoriously.

Although I am a Christian and do trust the Lord, I find I am becoming very nervous and irritable—often about quite trifling things. I feel I have just about reached the breaking point and cannot cope any longer. What do you think is wrong with me?

More than one thing may be wrong, but it sounds as though you are physically run-down and have got into a state of nervous exhaustion. In that case you need to relax a bit more, to find time for some recreation, and if possible to get away for a few days' holiday.

Remember that as a Christian it is your duty to keep yourself as fit as possible, spiritually *and* physically. You cannot be the best for God if you drive yourself to the point where you are practically dropping with fatigue and something within you is about to snap.

When the apostles returned from their first preaching tour the Lord Jesus said to them, "Come ye yourselves apart, and rest awhile" (Mark 6:31). He recognized that they had bodies as well as souls. He knew their need of rest if they were to be of further service to Him.

There is something else I would ask you to remember. When Jesus called those apostles to come apart and rest awhile, He was inviting them to spend time in communion with Him. I wonder how that applies to you? Are you finding time each day for fellowship with the Lord?

Nothing so restores mental equilibrium as regular, daily prayer. Try the apostolic formula: "Careful for nothing, prayer for everything, thankful for anything—and *then* the peace of God will be yours" (Philippians 4:6–7).

I have a chronic intestinal trouble which the doctor says is caused by worry. He tells me to relax, but how can I when the success of my business and the employment of 5000 men and women depend upon me?

Your question indicates that you believe your work is important. If that is true, it is God's work. He has given it to you. And He will help you do it, if you ask Him.

Begin each day by saying the Lord's Prayer. When you come to the words "Give us this day our daily bread" remember that Jesus told us to ask only for the needs of one day. Most of our worries come from being too concerned about the future. When Christ was in Galilee He gave Himself entirely to the work there. He didn't wear Himself out by worrying what would happen to Him in Jerusalem when it was time for Him to go there. He knew that when future trials came, he could meet them with the Father's help.

In the life of Christ we find our example. Trust in God. Each morning ask Him to guide you in the decisions you must make that day. Every hour take time to send a minute prayer to Heaven. You may have felt like a deep-sea diver who is suffocating for want of air. Prayer is the lifeline that brings divine oxygen to your lungs.

Then when you go from your place of business, leave all thoughts of your work behind. Enjoy your family and friends. Take time to read the Bible daily. Take some recreation each week.

Jesus said: "Take no thought for the morrow: for the morrow shall take thought for the things of itself" (Matthew 6:34). Do this. Live one day at a time, trusting in God, and you'll find no need to worry.

I have been mentally sick for several years, though I am much better now. During this sickness I made several sincere vows to God which have been a burden to keep. Now my life is miserable trying to keep them. I fear God's wrath should I break my promises. Tell me what to do.

The Bible has much to say about vows. On the one hand, God warns against making idle vows and says, "When thou vowest a vow unto God, defer not to pay, for He hath no pleasure in fools. Better not to have vowed than to vow and not pay" (Ecclesiastes 5:4). Scriptures such as this one are intended by God to give us the strongest warning against making meaningless vows without intending to complete them.

But God is forever an understanding God. He is quick to discern the intentions of His children and consider motives in what we do. Your comfort must be found in another Scripture which says: "Like as a father pitieth his children, so the Lord pitieth them that fear Him. For He knoweth our frame; He remembereth that we are dust" (Psalm 103:13). None of God's demands are unreasonable, nor will He hold you to the vow when it was made in sincerity, but when you were perhaps not mentally responsible. The Bible says that "His commands are not grievous" (I John 5:3). Commit your problem to Him as to a loving father and let your mind be at rest.

I'm crippled with arthritis and I'm useless. What's the good of living?

God doesn't think you're useless. He needs all kinds of people to do His work. He needs the quick, and the slow. He needs the strong, and the weak. I know a boy without any arms, who paints with his toes. The lad's courage has inspired many to forget their handicaps. If you are cheerful and patient when in pain, you are witnessing for Christ.

A retired minister spends three hours each day writing friendly notes to those in trouble. His messages bring courage and comfort to thousands every year.

God has something special for you to do. Of course it won't be the same type of work you once did. Ask God how you can serve Him, and He will tell you.

We can't understand why illness comes, but when we suffer we must still trust our Heavenly Father. Then we have more time for prayer than ever before. Pray for others as well as yourself. Pray for those in positions of authority. Pray for peace and justice. Even when lying flat on your back, you can pray. And no prayer is ever wasted.

This is one way you can now labor for Christ and His Kingdom.

A few years after my marriage, I yielded to temptation and was unfaithful to my wife for about two years. I know I was wrong, and although I have been true to my marriage vows since then, I have been worried lest God would not forgive my sin.

Few sins are dealt with as severely as the sin of adultery, according to the Bible.

We do not in any way suggest that sin is not serious business. But after facing the seriousness of it, we can never stop short of pointing out that God is a forgiving God. Your sin was so serious that it called for the suffering and death of the Son of God. But His death was so adequate and sufficient that because He died and rose again, God can offer complete forgiveness to every repentant sinner.

But I will tell you the conditions under which God could not forgive you and would not forgive you. If your repentance is not genuine, and if you would like forgiveness while continuing in your sin, then you make it impossible for God to offer you His pardon and restore you to fellowship with Himself, for He is a holy God.

I lived with my husband two months before we were married. I have asked God to forgive me, but I don't feel that He has. Is there any hope for me ever feeling good and clean again? Is divorce the answer?

Yes, of course there is hope for you. You will remember Jesus' tolerance and understanding toward the adulteress to whom He said: "Neither do I condemn thee, go thy way and sin no more." He forgave Mary Magdalene, and the woman at Jacob's well, and they were both guilty of breaking the Seventh Commandment.

Divorce in your case is out of the question and certainly is not the answer to your problem. You must believe God's promises and claim them as your very own. He said: "If we confess our sins, He is faithful and just to forgive our sins, and to cleanse us from all unrighteousness" (I John 1:9). You have let this past sin prey on your mind. Now, you must focus your attention away from the past, and on God's promises for the present. He stands ready, not only to forgive you, but to cleanse you from "all unrighteousness." But, you must claim this cleansing as religiously as you have held on to your guilt. As the negative, defeatist thoughts are crowded out of your mind by the positive, regenerating thoughts engendered by God's Spirit, you will find release from the past which has haunted you. May God give you faith to step out on His sure promises.

I am worried about my future. I left my husband and ran off with another man. Now I know I did wrong but it is too late. Is there any hope or way out?

You are but one of many who has made a grave mistake. You have sinned against your husband; against this other man; against yourself; and, against God. But Christ came into the world to save sinners and He came to save you. I do not know how He will untangle the twisted threads of your life but I know that He can and will if you truly repent and turn to Him for forgiveness and for help. The Bible is full of instances of forgiven sin and of God's promises to forgive sin. That is the Gospel message—Christ died for our sins. In the book of Isaiah, God says to Israel, and He says to us today: "Come now, and let us reason together, saith the Lord: though your sins be as scarlet, they shall be as wool." One day Jesus was talking to a woman who had sinned as you have. Evidently He saw the sorrow and shame she felt and knew that in her heart she wanted forgiveness and to lead a clean life. He said to her: "Neither do I condemn thee: go, and sin no more." Turn to Him in full repentance and remember that He loved you so much He died for you. He will not turn you down but will forgive you and make your heart white and clean once more. He will also show you what you will have to do in the future.

Can God forgive an unwed mother?

Of course He can, and will! I used to think that unwed
mothers were the hard, immoral type. But one day I visited
a home where these girls were brought. I was surprised to
note the look of innocence upon most of their faces. They
were young, unsophisticated girls who had inadvertently
fallen into sin.

The Seventh Commandment is just one of ten. The sin of
immorality, although God loathes it as He does all sin,
is no worse than lying, cheating, or stealing. We see examples
all through the Bible of God forgiving this sin. Mary Magdalene, the adulteress, and the woman of Jacob's well had
all crossed the line of propriety, but they all found forgiveness in Christ.

Some of the great Christians of history have been persons with dark pasts. St. Augustine, John Newman, and a
host of others were able to speak the language of sinners,
for they had been on both sides of the street. The word
Christ has for persons who have broken the Seventh Commandment is: "Neither do I condemn thee; go thy way
and sin no more."

*My husband has confessed to me that he was having an
immoral affair with his secretary, and has since accepted
Christ and has joined the church. But I find myself filled
with suspicion and doubts about him. How can I conquer
these thoughts that have all but ruined my happiness?*

This sort of situation always poses problems that have
no easy solution. Your husband's confession was a shock to
you, and of course at the time you forgave him. But forgiveness involves the act of forgetting. The Bible says that when
God forgives us, "He remembers our sins against us no more."
It is impossible to genuinely forgive and still harbor resent-
ments. The person who says "I forgive you but I can't forget
it" doesn't know the meaning of forgiveness.

You don't mention that your husband has given you
any cause for suspicion. The fact that he confessed his
wrong was proof in itself that he was sincere, for it takes

much courage to do this. You must pray for the grace of forgiveness. An unforgiving spirit can wreck your spiritual life, and could also ruin your home. As long as your husband gives evidence of living for Christ, you should put away any suspicion, for doubting him at this point without cause could discourage him and bring calamity to your marriage. May God give you grace for your difficult assignment.

I have been keeping company with a man for fifteen years. We have broken the Seventh Commandment many times. I could have married him long ago, but did not want to leave my home. Now we are planning to marry. What chance of happiness do we have?

Yours is not an ideal setting for married happiness, but I sincerely hope you can get your lives straightened out. To begin with, your relationship with this man seems to have been on a purely biological level, and sex is certainly not the only ingredient of marital bliss. In fact, marriages that are based on this alone are doomed to failure. The divorce courts are full of disillusioned people who mistakenly thought that animal magnetism was true love.

Do you love this man, and are you both willing to take God into your marriage partnership? The Bible says: "What God hath joined together let no man put asunder." The only really sound marriages are those based on mutual respect. In the light of your continuously breaking the Seventh Commandment, do you two have respect, admiration, and love for each other?

Marriage may ease your conscience a bit, but if I were you two, I would bow before God together and ask Him to forgive you for deliberately breaking His law, and jeopardizing your reputations, and your influence in the community. He has said: "Though your sins be as scarlet, they shall be as wool." With God you can be happy.

After many years of unhappy married life, my husband died leaving me a widow. After his death I lived a very wicked life, satisfying all of the physical passions. I knew it was wrong, but couldn't seem to help myself. For several years I have wanted to be a Christian but somehow have never felt that God could forgive all of this sin. It is hard to believe that He could forgive that kind of life. Is there anything I can do to be saved?

As men we make differences between small and large sins. God does not do this. To Him, any sin however slight is so offensive that it must be treated as the greatest of sins. For example, in Galatians 5:19–21 you will notice that fornication and jealousy are considered almost the same. When Christ died, He died to make atonement for every sin. The Bible says: "For if a man is in Christ, he becomes a new person altogether: the past is finished and gone; everything has become fresh and new. All this is God's doing, for He has reconciled us to Himself through Jesus Christ, and has made us agents of the reconciliation. God was in Christ, personally reconciling the world to Himself, not counting their sins against them" (II Corinthians 5:17, Phillips' translation).

The moment you believe in Christ, your past is completely erased and done away with. Accept this provision through faith in Christ. In that acceptance you are born again. From that time on everything is new.

A friend of mine, who is not a believer, has been suffering all her life with a drunken husband, wayward children, and several serious accidents. Don't you think that some people have their hell here on earth?

The Bible says that "He maketh the sun to shine and the rain to fall on the just and the unjust alike." God does not protect some and leave others to the forces of some unknown power or circumstance. He is aware of the circumstances and details of our lives. In this life, we share alike in suffering and in pleasure. What the future has for each individual depends upon his relationship to Jesus Christ. Suffering and disappointment are often God's signals to us, reminding us of our problem and of our condition. If we see such things in the light of the Bible, then we understand that no one has his hell here, but that certainly there is a heaven for those who have in this life confessed Christ and a hell for those who have refused Him. "He that hath the Son hath life, but he that hath not the Son shall not see life, but the wrath of God abideth on him." No matter what this life holds for you, make sure that for eternity you have settled the problem of sin and salvation through Jesus Christ.

Chapter 13

The Way You Look and Act

Do you think that a Christian woman should wear revealing clothing such as low-neck dresses and tight shorts?

The Bible has actually very little to say about the clothing we wear. Most likely it is because the primary message of the Bible is concerned with the redemption of sinners through Christ. Its message emphasizes the Cross and the Resurrection of our Lord Jesus and how men are saved through His work on our behalf.

But the Bible does mention briefly such matters. Paul to Timothy established a principle that applies to ladies' fashions in every generation. He said: "I desire . . . that women adorn themselves in modest apparel." Peter supplemented that by saying that the adornment should be "The hidden man of the heart, in the incorruptible apparel of a meek and quiet spirit which is in the sight of God of great price." It all depends upon whether the primary objective in dress is to appear tastefully dressed or to excite those of the opposite sex. The Christian will always elect to appear Godly and to adorn the Gospel by every appearance.

While I was in the service, I acquired some tattoos of which I am not now proud—especially since I have become a Christian. Will God hold this against me, even if I can have these tattoos removed successfully?

138

After we have confessed our sins, turned from them and trusted in Christ as our Saviour, God does not hold anything against us. It is sin in the heart which separates us from God, not marks on our bodies. And while hard to understand, once we have accepted what Christ did for us on the Cross, not only are our sins forgiven, they are also forgotten. Ask God to free you of a morbid living in the past and just rejoice that you are now a new man, made new by the One who died for you. The marks on your body may remain but some day you will have a glorified body which will be perfect in every respect. I know a man who has many tattoo marks on his body. If anyone asks him about them he says: "I got them when I was serving the devil, but I belong to someone else now and He is the Lord of my body, soul, and spirit."

Is there any difference between pride in one's accomplishments and personal pride, such as one's appearance? According to the Bible it seems to be a sin; but without pride there seems to be no reason for careful grooming, good housekeeping, etc.

Nowhere in the Bible do I read that God puts a premium on slovenliness or disarray. However, the Bible places the emphasis on spiritual sloveliness, rather than physical. It is possible for a person to be impeccable in his attire and person, and yet be slovenly in his morals and conduct. On the other hand, a person of modest means may not win the name of the "best-dressed" man in town, but his character can be irreproachable, and that is what counts.

"God does not look upon the outward appearance, but upon the heart." But at the same time, I believe that a neat, clean, well-groomed Christian is more impressive than a slovenly one. The saying "Cleanliness is next to Godliness" has a lot to recommend it. It would be poor policy to keep the inside of our houses immaculately clean, but let tin cans and garbage accumulate in the yard. By the same token, if Christ has cleansed our hearts, the least that we can do to keep our bodies, which are the temples of the Spirit, clean, neat, and presentable.

I am a woman with an attractive figure. Is there any reason why I should not dress to show it off? My husband intimates that I dress "sexy" to attract other men. While it is true that other men pay attention to me at a social gathering, I can't see what is wrong in displaying a woman's charms.

Has it ever occurred to you that a woman can have other attractive features besides an attractive body? You deserve no credit for nature's endowments, so why should you strut like a peacock over something you had no control over? Strive rather to be a lady in every sense of the word. I have seen women who were not especially attractive physically, who could charm a group by their winsomeness and grace.

If you think of yourself as just a beautiful animal, you are bound to neglect the beautification of your mind and spirit. In order to be well-rounded human beings, we must develop symmetrically—not just in one direction. Don't be a proverbial "dumb blonde" (not that all blondes are dumb), but strive to develop your mind by knowledge, and your soul by spiritual grace. Christ alone can give a woman true, lasting charm and beauty.

Chapter 14

Friends, Relatives, and Neighbors

My husband and I took some of our relatives into our home to help them over a rough spot. We even led them to the Saviour and we believe they are genuinely Christian. But now they just stay here and we don't really have a home. The man won't work, and the woman helps just a little. We don't want to send them away, because it might hurt their spiritual life. What can we do?

If one's spiritual life is such a delicate thing, it is not really a work of God at all. Those that God has saved from their former way of life and given the gift of salvation are quite rugged. In fact, one of the basic responsibilities of every child of God is to work. Paul wrote: "If any man will not work, neither let him eat" (II Thessalonians 3:10).

Industry is becoming to a Christian, and this relative of yours must be made to face some of these facts. In another letter Paul wrote: "But we exhort you, brethren, that ye abound more and more, and that ye study to be quiet, and to do your own business, and to work with your hands even as we charged you; that ye may walk becomingly toward them that are without, and may have need of nothing" (I Thessalonians 4:10–12).

As Christians we ought to help one another, but if your relatives are able-bodied, they should be given a date when they must be on their own again.

141

A couple of years ago I became estranged from my church through the sharp tongue of one of the ladies. I withdrew completely. What should be done with people of sharp tongues and sarcasm?

The best thing to do is to ignore their remarks. The Bible says: "Love suffereth long, and is kind; love . . . is not easily provoked, thinketh no evil" (I Corinthians 13:4, 5). It isn't easy to do this, but if we want to be followers of Jesus we must try. For two long years you have been poisoning your mind and body with resentment. Stop now. Follow Christ's example and pray for the one who spitefully used you. See her as Christ sees her. When you meet her, act as if you had forgotten her caustic remarks. Better still, fill your mind so full of love that there will be no room for peevishness.

Next Sunday go back to your church. Once more worship God in your accustomed place. As you enter the church, center your thoughts on Christ. If the idea comes to your mind that some in the congregation are not Christlike, remember that you have failed Him, too. You will find new joy when you obey Jesus' command: "Bless them that curse you, and pray for them which despitefully use you" (Luke 6:28).

My brother is about to marry a girl who is totally unfit for him. Is there any way I can show him his error and keep him from this fatal step? I love him and have made a good home for him since our parents died.

Probably you will never think any girl is good enough for your brother. He is without doubt a wonderful young man. But if he is such a fine fellow, why don't you trust his judgment in this matter? I think you would do more harm than good to interfere. Your problem is with yourself, for it may mean the breakup of your home. You are a very dependent person and now your security is being taken away. Everyone desires security and the sense of being needed. I would like to suggest to you that your lost feeling may be a good thing for you. It should teach you that whenever we lean upon some person for support, we are in danger of serious disappointment. God has given us all that instinctive dependence so that we might come to depend upon Him. Let your human loss be a real gain. Let God have the part He should have in your life. Then you will not only be adjusted to your problem, but you will discover a new joy that comes through personal faith. Christ can become "a friend that sticketh closer than a brother."

I am writing you for all of us children whose mother recently died. Now Father is planning to remarry, and we know we can never get along with a stepmother. Can't something be done to help us?

It is unfortunate that the word "stepmother" has too often fallen into disrepute. Some of the most noble women I know are stepmothers. To become a stepmother is much more difficult than being a mother. The love of her mate must be divided between many people, and she must do a tedious job of family "wire-walking."

You say that you know you can never get along with a stepmother. It is this preconceived sort of attitude that usually rules out any chances of happiness in a situation like yours. With this in your minds, the best woman in the world couldn't get along with you.

I am deeply sympathetic with you children, for you have sustained a great loss. But we have to take life where we find it and proceed from there. I suggest you think of the self-sacrifice of the woman who loves your father well enough to share her love with his first wife's children, and who is willing to submerge her own identity, her own desires, and her own freedom in your family situation. Think it over, and I'm sure that although I can't do anything to help you, you children can do a lot to help yourselves by changing your attitude to the idea of a "stepmother."

There is a woman in our community who runs around openly with a married man. She is forty and he is thirty. On Sunday she goes to church and pretends to be the best one there.

People are getting tired of the way she acts. Don't you think someone should talk to her?

I think Someone *is* talking to her. Her conscience is doubtless talking to her, her better judgment is talking to her, and I'm sure God is talking to her. The fact that she goes to church is not so much an indication of her hypocrisy as it is her hunger for something more satisfying in life. If I were you I would be slow to gossip about this woman, lest you place yourself in the position of those ancient Pharisees who wanted to stone the adulterous woman. Jesus said: "Let him that is without sin cast the first stone." And they all slipped away from the scene.

It is easy to get all steamed up about someone else's sin. That is human and natural. But what we forget is that "All have sinned and come short of the glory of God." If you do talk to this woman, do it in love and in the Spirit of Christ. She is no worse than the woman at Jacob's well to whom Christ gave the water of life.

Above all, the people in the church who are concerned ought to covenant together to pray for this poor sinful woman!

I play golf with a friend of mine and I'm sorry to say that he cheats. I seldom win, and if I do it's because I have bypassed a few of the rules myself. Why do grown men resort to such tactics just to win a game?

Your question would be amusing if it were not so tragically sad. I happen to play the game of golf and like it because it's so unpredictable and challenging. Of all games, golf is supposed to be a game of honor. It is a game for gentlemen, and if the rules are not observed it ceases to be any fun for anyone. In fact, it ceases to be golf.

When anyone wants to win so badly that he resorts to cheating, he is missing the whole point of the game. If he wins he has really lost, for he has lost that feeling of honor and good sportsmanship that is the point of every fair athletic contest.

I'm afraid that this trait of dishonesty is almost becoming

a national characteristic with us. We see it in politics, in business, in TV, and now, in the grand old game of golf.

Grantland Rice once wrote a poem that I would like you to read with your friend. It ends like this:

> *And when that One Great Scorer comes*
> *To write against your name;*
> *He writes not that you won or lost,*
> *But how you played the game.*

Chapter 15

How to Make Wrong Things Right

My husband and I are Christian people, and have tried to have a home that would please the Lord. We have some relatives who come to visit once in a while, and when they come they practice some of their bad habits that trouble us greatly. We would hate to have some of our friends find them in our house. Do you think it would be right to invite them to leave or to inform them of our regulations?

In the many times they have visited, have you tried definitely to help them spiritually? Perhaps they come to you in the hope that they will receive some spiritual help. Perhaps they are ignorant of your standards, or at least perhaps they do not know why you have standards at all. Your house might become a vacuum if you just abstain from things you consider to be bad. Make it a positive thing in which there is a spiritual influence brought to bear upon all who visit you. Prayer over the meals, a discussion of the Bible without argument, a rehearsal of the goodness of God in your lives would be most appropriate. You can attempt to be so tactful that you fail to make a contact. Remember that even Jesus ate with sinners, but He always met them on His conditions, and He never lowered His standards. I do not recall that He was ever ashamed of being found in their company, for He lifted people but never was lowered by them.

146

I have caused a former friend much suffering through financial losses and terrible injustices I have committed for my own financial gain. What can I do to be forgiven for my awful crime?

Your question projects a dark picture, but the fact that you realize you have done wrong shows there is hope. The Bible gives a precise formula for people in your plight: "If thou bring thy gift to the altar, and there rememberest that thy brother hath aught against thee; leave thy gift before the altar, first be reconciled to thy brother and then come and offer thy gift."

Go to the person you have wronged. In humility ask him to forgive you. Then assure him that you will repay all that you owe him in due time. Then, and only then, will you be prepared to give your life to God. Too many people try to climb into the kingdom of God over the accumulated debris of an ugly and sinful past. God can forgive the sins of the heart, but wrongs done against others must be made right if we are to have peace with God.

When Zaccheus, the crooked tax-collector, came face to face with Christ and his own wickedness he said: "If I have wronged any man, I will restore him fourfold." When he said that, Jesus said: "Today I will abide at thy house." Christ comes to live with every man who sincerely vows to straighten out his life in the way God requires.

Some time ago I served as the treasurer of the church. From time to time I took small sums of money, intending to repay it as soon as possible. Now another man has been elected to the office and I am ashamed to tell him what I did, but I must repay the amount to balance the record. Can you help me with a suggestion?

You must clear your conscience and keep the record straight. You cannot have peace until you do so. I would suggest that you take into your confidence the pastor of the church. Your problem is certainly one that has some spiritual implications, and you can be sure that he will not betray your confidence.

There is no question about what must be done. It is merely a matter of procedure, and it would be the proper procedure to confide in your pastor. He will be the kind of person you need to include in such a problem. In fact, he has much at stake in every such problem. The Bible tells us that we should submit to them who have such responsibility "As they must give account, that they may do it with joy, and not grief: for that is profitable for you" (Hebrews 13:17).

Some years ago my sister and I had a fuss over the division of our mother's property and we have not visited each other or spoken since. I still believe I was right but I am truly unhappy about it.

It is probable that your sister is just as unhappy about this as you are and that she also thinks she was right. It is my guess that you both were wrong and that you have been acting like spoiled children, rather than as adults. Could any possible division of your mother's things in your favor have made all of this unhappiness worthwhile? Can you take one single thing with you when you die? The thing for you to do is phone, write, or go to see your sister and ask her forgiveness. You may be rebuffed but my guess is that she will welcome you with open arms. I would also go right to the root of your trouble and offer to make any adjustment which she may desire. If you do this in true love I believe you both will find a new joy and peace in your lives. Incidentally, family rows like you describe take all of the joy out of life. Take the first step and make amends for what has happened. It may seem hard at first but I believe it will bring you great happiness.

Some time ago I cheated in an examination in college. The rule of the college is that we lose credit for any course in which we cheat. Now it bothers my conscience, but if I report my action, I am in danger of losing my degree from the college. Would it be right for me to just let this matter alone, and perhaps I can eventually overcome my troubled conscience?

God gave each one of us a conscience for a reason. An enlightened conscience is our best guide. But if you stifle it and refuse to listen to it, you will soon render it ineffective. You are in danger of destroying its voice. You know that your action was wrong. There is only one way to clear up the matter. It would be much better to take that course over again at some convenient time than to disobey the voice of your conscience. I cannot tell what the college authorities will do about it. You must do whatever is right no matter what the consequences may be. I am sure that the knowledge that you have acted in the light God has given you will more than repay whatever you stand to lose through such action.

Some months ago I passed on a bit of innocent gossip about a person who is truly my friend. I did not mean any harm but recently this has become the basis of a scandal, and I feel guilty and sorry. What can I do to make amends?

Gossip, even about incidents that seem very minor, is a serious sin. We can never recover our words and they always grow and become distorted. There is a game sometimes played where people pass on some remark to the next person in line, and doing so in a whisper, by the time the story reaches the end of the line it is very different. This illustrates what happens when we gossip. It is like taking a bag of feathers and dropping one at a time while walking down the road. We can never walk back and pick up all of the feathers. In your case the Christian thing to do is to go to your friend and confess what you have done, ask for forgiveness and then do all that you possibly can to tell others and right the wrong. The Bible says: "A tale-bearer revealeth secrets; but he that is of a faithful spirit concealeth a matter." In this, as in all other matters, the Bible gives us wisdom for daily living. Try telling others some of the good things you know of individuals; you will be surprised how happy it will make you, and all concerned.

For some time I have been stealing small amounts of money from the company that employs me. Now that I have come to know Christ, I feel that I must do something about this. I'm afraid to tell my employer lest I lose my position, yet I cannot live with my conscience troubling me as it now does. What would you suggest?

I think you will find that every employer will respect you for making an honest confession. Even though your life up until this time has been one of deception, yet the confession will convince him more than ever that something has taken place in your life and I feel that he will come to regard you as one of the most dependable workers he has. Even more important than clearing your own conscience, it is the thing you should do in order to give you the best possible opportunity to tell what God can do in the life of one who turns to Him. Having done what is pleasing to God, you can always leave the results to Him. We will pray that you will have courage to do what you know is the right thing.

Some time ago I drove a car for a gang which robbed a filling station. Since then I have become a Christian and my conscience hurts me. What should I do?

In the eyes of the law you were an accomplice in a crime. In God's eyes you were just as guilty as those who did the actual robbing. My advice to you is to go to see the judge in the place where this robbery took place and tell him the whole story. Explain the difficulty you have in involving other people in a crime. Tell him you have become a Christian and want to do the right thing, taking any punishment which you should take. Ask his advice and take that advice. It would probably be wise for you to talk this over with your pastor first and, if he is willing, take him with you to talk to the judge. This is a hard decision and it may mean that you will have to suffer for it, but it will bring peace to your soul and enable you to witness for the Saviour you have put your trust in. I have a friend who had much the same experience you have had and he made a full confession.

he result is that God is using him in a very wonderful
ay today.

*have been in prison for four years for robbery. Since
*ming here I have been converted. But I did not commit
*e robbery for which I was convicted and I do not know
*ho did it. However, I was guilty of another robbery about
*hich they know nothing. What shall I do when I get out
xt year?

s a Christian you owe it to the authorities to confess the
evious robbery and ask for mercy. Then you owe it to the
*e or ones whom you robbed to repay that which you stole.
is may take a lot of hard work but it is the right thing
do and you will get great satisfaction in doing it. The
tlook of a Christian must be different from other people
d we have to learn to take things which come to us as
rist would have us do. In making confession to the author-
es and restitution to the ones you have wronged you can
orify God and at the same time He may use your actions
win someone else to Him.

*y wife and I were never legally married. She is what I
ink you would call a "common-law wife." After living
this country for a number of years our friends have told*
that we are living in adultery and not truly married at all.
hat is your judgment in this matter?

. our social system in the United States, we have come to
nsider marriage as being legal and binding only when it
performed by a person who is really authorized to per-
rm such a service, either a minister or a justice of the
ace. There are many foreign countries where this is not
e case. Certainly, the many people who have been married
cording to the customs of other countries cannot be con-
lered to be living in adultery. Marriage is a spiritual thing
fore it is a physical and legal matter. It is the agreement
hearts and minds to come together under God for a life-
ne relationship. You have been faithful to each other
rough the many years that you have lived together and

God has blessed your relationship with fine children. I would certainly not advocate a return to common-law marriages, but we know too well that there are many marriages that are legally correct and yet there is no love existing and there is much unfaithfulness. It is only God who in the final analysis can unite a man and woman in marriage together.

I would, however, urge you to get legally married, immediately. Make it a time of dedication to each other and God.

I understand that the Bible tells us to forgive our enemies many times. Although I have tried to forgive a certain person for a wrong done deliberately, I simply cannot. I have no other enemies. Do you think God will judge me for having just this one person that I cannot forgive?

Forgiveness is natural for the Christian and is contrary to the non-Christian. Even the non-Christian has friends and loved ones, but he loves them because they love him in return. Here is the distinctiveness of the Christian life. Jesus said: "Love your enemies, do good to those that despitefully use you," and on another occasion He said that they should forgive until seventy times seven. God can and will give you a forgiving spirit when you accept His forgiveness through Jesus Christ. When you do, you will realize that He has forgiven you so much that you will desire to forgive any wrong. In the world, a policy of getting even with the other fellow is generally accepted. Among Christians, it is the policy of enduring wrong for the sake of Christ and forgiving that men might through us discover the grace of God in forgiving the sinner.

rayer Power Works Every Hour

y problem is that I cannot concentrate when I pray. In
her matters I am quite able to keep my mind from wan-
ring but not when I kneel to pray. Is there something
ong with me?

ere is not necessarily anything wrong with you. This
s the problem the disciples had in the Garden of
thsemane. They went to sleep when they had been com-
nded to "watch and pray." Of all the activity of the
ristian life, prayer is the most difficult. The Bible even
ints this out, saying that "We know not how to pray as
ought."

Someone has said: "Satan trembles when the weakest saint
upon his knees." When we get to Heaven, I am convinced
will be amazed at our prayerlessness. Prayer can move
untains. Thus Satan will do all in his power to distract
u. You may never be entirely free from distraction in
ayer, but you can improve by quoting Psalms, using
ayer helps. Remember also that prayer is a two-way con-
rsation. Be still and listen for the voice of God. Most of
want to do too much talking in prayer. God has promised
ecial help in the matter of prayer. "And in like manner
e Spirit helpeth our infirmities: for we know not what we
ould pray for as we ought: but the Spirit himself maketh
ercession for us" (Romans 8:26). No matter what your
oblem, don't get discouraged. Continue to pray.

Is it more meaningful to kneel while you pray? Is it ju
an expression of humbleness, or are one's prayers mor
likely to be heard when kneeling?

It is not the posture of the body, but the attitude of th
heart that counts when we pray. The Bible speaks of bowin
in prayer, kneeling, on the face before God, standing, si
ting, and walking. The important thing is not the positio
of the body but the condition of the soul. If the heart i
attuned to God, one can pray in any posture imaginable

Jesus prayed sitting, standing, kneeling, and in a pron
position. Moses often fell on his face to pray. Daniel fre
quently kneeled. The disciples were sitting in the uppe
room when the Holy Spirit descended upon them in answe
to prayer. Ahab prayed with his face between his knees.

There are times when I like to kneel in prayer. There ar
other times when it seems more natural to sit or stand.
don't believe there is any special virtue in any particula
posture. God doesn't look upon the outward appearance, bu
upon the heart.

Is it always necessary to pray for long periods of time
maintain a spiritual outlook?

It is not the length of the prayer that is important. Do yo
think God is persuaded by long prayers or by the earnes
ness with which we pray? Put it on the level of the humar
What makes the strongest impression on you? Is it the lon
but indifferent request or the terse but earnest plea of on
who has a strong desire? I am sure you can see that it
the condition of the heart and the definiteness of the reque
that make the difference. Jesus said, "When you pray, c
not as the heathen do, using vain repetition." The simple ar
direct request in Jesus' name will accomplish far more tha
millions of halfhearted and indefinite words. Finally, pra
expecting. God knows when you pray without hope of a
answer. You cannot pray unless you pray with hope.

It is interesting to note that Jesus often prayed all ni
in private but His public prayers were very brief.

*a public function where there are people of different
faiths, should a Christian pray and not pray in the name of
Christ?*

I presume that the question is taking into consideration the
possibility of praying in the name of Christ offending some
of another faith. The real consideration is whether we shall
offend God. Christ has specifically told us to make our prayers in His name. To omit His name for the sake of a supposed courtesy to others is a very dangerous procedure. An
American citizen will proudly admit his American citizenship,
regardless of who is present. Should Christians refuse to
admit their Christian citizenship for fear of offending others?
Your question is of considerable importance because the New
Testament teaches so plainly that man has access to God in
and through the name of His Son. That is why we end our
prayers, "For Christ's sake." I have a friend who recently
had a caller. The young man standing at the door (a total
stranger to him) said: "I saw your son out in New Mexico
last week." He was immediately welcomed into the home, not
because of who he was but for the sake of the son in the
West whom they had not seen for some time. In the same
way we are "welcome" to God only because we know His
Son.

*How can I get close to God? Praying to Him is like praying
to a brick wall; and although countless prayers of mine have
been answered, it seems that my prayers just slide into the
blackness of I-don't-know-where. Do you think you could
possibly help me?*

I'm afraid you are trying to use God as a genie, as a kind of
Aladdin's lamp proposition. You say that countless prayers
have been answered. That seems to me like a pretty good
average. God answers all of our prayers, but in His wisdom,
He often answers some of them with a "no."

Prayer is not using God; it is more often to get us in a
position where God can use us.

I watched the deck hands on the great liner, *United States,*
as they docked that ship in New York Harbor. First, they

threw out a rope to the men on the dock. Then inside the boat the great motors went to work and pulled on that great cable. But oddly enough, the pier wasn't pulled out to the ship; but the ship was pulled snugly up to the pier.

Prayer is the rope that pulls God and man together. But it doesn't pull God down to us: it pulls us to Him. We must learn to say with Christ, the master of the art of prayer: "Not my will; but thine be done."

We know people who won't help a living thing. They drink they swear, and they lie . . . and yet they seem to prosper Is this the kind of life God wants? Does He answer the prayers of the wicked? I pray, but despair of ever having wealth like other people have. Please help me and make me believe there is a God.

I detect a tone of bitterness and resentment in your letter and I am sorry for you. You should not envy the material prosperity of people who are spiritually impoverished! Jesus said: "Seek ye first the kingdom of God and His righteousness, and all these things shall be added unto you."

Resentment and bitterness are hell's greatest destroyers of human happiness. They canker the spirit, and will rob you of the joy you are entitled to. Nowhere do we read in the Bible that the scales of life are in perfect balance. Jesus spoke of the greedy rich man who had much, and the good Lazarus who had nothing. But in the afterlife, their positions were reversed, and in due time they were both rewarded

I suggest that you obey the commandment "Thou shalt not covet," and give your time and attention to accumulating spiritual treasure—the kind that will endure throughout eternity. "Seek first the kingdom of God."

Why is it that so many prayers are unanswered? In fact, wonder if there is anything to prayer at all.

There are many reasons why prayer is not answered. God is by no means obliged to answer every prayer for every person

he Bible tells us that sometimes prayers are not answered
ecause we nourish and cherish sin in our hearts. Again it
lls us that it is because we desire things to consume on our-
lves, in other words, selfish reasons. But most of all, you
hould remember that God promises to answer prayers for
ertain things, not just anything. He will answer the prayer
f any sinner who prays for pardon in the name of Jesus
Romans 10:13). He will give Himself in His fullness to any
eliever who sincerely desires His fullness (Luke 11:14).
e promises to cleanse all the sins of any child who comes to
im confessing his sins (I John 1:9), He will give wisdom
nd spiritual insight to those who acknowledge their lack
nd who sincerely desire such wisdom (James 1:5). If you
re a fully yielded Christian, and commit your whole life to
im, He promises to give you even the whole desire of your
eart (Psalm 37:4, 5). This is a simple formula, but it will
ncourage you to pray according to His will. Then you will
ot need to feel that God ignores your request.

Of course, there are many other prayers that God answers
hat are not mentioned in the Bible—if we pray according
o His will in Christ's name with a motive to glorify God.

*have been praying that my husband would become a Chris-
an and stop drinking. Can he be saved through my prayers
f he doesn't pray about it? I can't talk to him about it be-
ause he becomes violently angry when I do, and then he
ust drinks all the more.*

ertainly God can answer your prayers to bring about the
onversion of your husband, but don't be more concerned
bout discovering a cure for his drinking than in the con-
ersion of a lost soul. It is doubtful if selfish prayers are
ven much consideration in heaven. In the Bible it is writ-
en: "Ye ask, and receive not, because ye ask amiss, that ye
ay consume it in your pleasures" (James 4:3). As good as
rayer is, and as persistent as your prayers may be, it is
ssential for you to pray without any selfish motive.

But before your husband is truly converted he will have
pray. Everyone does. It is the simple prayer of a penitent

sinner who prays: "God be merciful to me, a sinner, and save me for Jesus' sake." The best part of it is that if he would do just that simple thing, God would accept him, not for his own goodness, but because salvation has been offered to all who trust in Christ.

It is also important that you don't nag your husband about this matter. The Bible says: "Likewise, ye wives, be in subjection to your own husbands; that if any obey not the word they also may without the word be won by the life of the wife" (I Peter 3:1).

My husband is in prison and we need him so. I've prayed that God would let him out, but so far my prayers have not been answered. Help me to know how to pray.

I am sorry that your husband is in prison. This is tragic, not only for him, but for his family. These things have a way of following a man down through the years, with the family bearing a big end of the reproach.

I can realize how badly you want your husband to be released, but may I remind you that God does not defy law and order. Obviously, your husband committed a wrong, and the Bible says, "Whatsoever a man soweth, that same shall he also reap."

You ask that I tell you how to pray. First, pray that grace will be given you to bear the reproach of being a convict's wife. This will not be easy. But, if you love him, which you obviously do, you will share in his suffering and embarrassment. Then, you should pray that this prison sentence will serve as a time of soul improvement for your husband. I receive letters from prisoners every week, telling how they discovered God behind the bars. Many men have come out of prison changed men. Pray that your husband might meet Christ there, and that the motives which led him into evil will be removed and remedied.

Then pray for the parole board, that if and when your husband has earned parole they will have wisdom as to how to deal with his case. May God bless you and give you patience and strength.

Can a person be saved by his mother's prayers?

A man who has a praying mother has a most cherished possession. I can think of no greater heritage than that of a saintly, praying mother. I have thanked God over and over again for a Christian mother.

However, though a mother's prayers may greatly influence a man's life and invoke the mercy of God on his behalf, it could hardly be said that a person can be saved by his mother's prayers. Our decision for Christ is one that we must make ourselves. Your mother's faithful prayers may have a great effect on you, but the ultimate and final decision is up to you. This is said with no intention of minimizing the value and effectiveness of faithful, praying parents.

Once in Northern Africa there was a Christian mother named Monica. She had a wayward son who was given to drunkenness and reveling. Before he left for a trip to Italy, she prayed all night that he might not go, but he went anyway. Later he wrote: "That night I stole away and she was left behind in weeping and prayer. And what, O Lord, was she with so many tears asking of Thee but that Thou wouldst not suffer me to sail? But Thou in the depth of thy counsels, knowing the main point of her desire, regardest not what she then asked, that Thou mightest accomplish the greater thing for which she was ever imploring Thee." Though long delayed, the mother's prayers were answered for that boy became the great Christian, St. Augustine.

Since God is infinitely busy with the great affairs of the universe, should we bother Him by praying about minor matters in our lives?

Your trouble seems to be that you have a wrong idea about God. Your conception of Him is far too small and limited. You are thinking of Him as though He were a finite being like yourself; whereas the God revealed to us in the Bible is a Being of infinite power and love. And the ultimate miracle is that He is *not* so busy with the great affairs of the universe that He cannot bother about these little lives of ours.

The mighty God who created the world and set the stars in motion is personally interested in every one of us. He loves us with an everlasting love. He gave His only begotten Son to die for our sins. The Cross is the measure and proof of how much He cares for us. And when by faith in Jesus Christ we respond to His love, we enter into a new and very personal relationship with Him as His children.

The Bible says concerning the Lord Jesus: "As many as received Him, to them gave He power to become the children of God, even to them that believe on His name" (John 1:12). When thus we receive Christ as our Lord and Saviour, God becomes known to us not only as the omnipotent Creator but as our loving Heavenly Father. And because He is our Father, He delights to hear and answer our prayers. He invites us to cast all our care upon Him because He cares for us.

How can I have faith that God will care about the comparatively trivial problems?

One of the striking truths in the teachings of Jesus is that God is concerned about and cares for the "little things." He said: "Are not two sparrows sold for a farthing? And one of them shall not fall to the ground without your Father. But the very hairs of your head are numbered. Fear ye not therefore, *ye are of more value than many sparrows.*"

Sparrows and hairs! What could be more insignificant? And yet His eye is on the sparrows, and He keeps record of the number of the hairs of your head! Since our minds are finite, it is difficult to grasp the ability of an infinite God to be interested in our trivial problems. But the Bible says that He is. It says, "Ye are of more value than many sparrows." It is reasonable to believe that God, who was concerned enough to send His Son to redeem us, is interested in the little burdens and cares that distress us. Just as an affectionate parent is interested in every little detail of his child, just so, only in greater measure, God cares for us. Peter, who had discovered God to be the God of little things, said: "Cast all your care upon Him, for He careth for you."

Sometimes when I am trying to pray I am distracted by all kinds of thoughts, both good and evil. They come racing through my mind until I feel that I know nothing at all about praying. This has made me doubt my salvation. Is it true that if I am saved these things will not happen to me?

There are very few people who know how to pray without interruption in thought. There are also very few who know exactly what to pray for. Romans 8:26 tells us that prayer is the great weakness of the average Christian, but it also tells us that we have help in our praying. In every other area of the Christian life we draw upon God's resources by recognizing our own weakness and insufficiency. I think you would find it true in your own prayer life that you will find new joy and new effectiveness in praying if you came to realize that you need the assistance of the Holy Spirit in your praying, and depend upon Him to prompt you and to direct your thoughts. Practice your prayer life in this way, and you will find it to be a richly rewarding experience. Spend plenty of time in your meditation upon the Scriptures for through His Word, God will encourage you to pray.

Chapter 17

Using Your Christian Citizenship

Don't you think that Christians should stay out of politics? Doesn't the Bible warn us "not to be entangled again with the yoke of bondage"?

I certainly do not think that Christians should be disinterested in the affairs of our government. Christ said: "Render unto Caesar the things that are Caesar's and unto God the things that are God's."

Nothing would please the racketeers, gangsters, and the underworld more than for all church people to stay away from the polls and to be uninformed about the goings on in Washington.

I would urge every Christian to vote and to show a keen interest in the politics of his community. I would even encourage him, if he felt so called, to take an active part in politics and to crusade for clean, honest, and upright handling of community affairs through good government.

The cliché "Politics is dirty" is plainly untrue. I know men who are in government who have high principles, fine motives, and unquestioned integrity. They have dedicated themselves to a life of public service because they sincerely want to serve their fellow men. While it is true that politics seem to attract some men of questionable principle, that fact makes it all the more imperative that good people everywhere cast their vote for the best candidates.

Should a Christian participate in defense measures of war involving the use of weapons, considering that his purpose is to kill other children of God?

First of all, the purpose of war is not to kill other children of God. If they are killed through the ravages of war, it is because they are members of a warring society and incidentally Christians. If war has any good purpose, it is to settle differences that men think cannot be settled by peaceful means. It is certainly not the Christian way of settling either individual or global problems.

On the other hand, we must accept our responsibility as citizens. A man may protest against war and criticize his government for becoming involved in war, but as a citizen, accepting the privileges and benefits of any government, he must also accept certain responsibilities. If we are in entire disagreement with our government, we can always elect to take our citizenship elsewhere. John the Baptist said one time when soldiers inquired of him concerning their duty: "Extort from no man by violence, neither accuse any one wrongfully; and be content with your wages." But he did not tell them that they must cease being soldiers.

A Christian would find it hard to be a loyal citizen in a nation that promoted warfare. We can thank God that we are part of a nation that seeks to solve all problems by peaceful means.

Recently I heard a preacher, while referring to politics during a sermon, make the statement that corrupt conditions in politics is the reason he has never registered or voted. Don't you think that Christians should vote?

Personally, I don't think people who are not even interested enough in what is going on in our country to register or vote are qualified to speak authoritatively on government. I know a great number of fine upstanding Christian statesmen. Perhaps there are some who are unethical and ulterior in their motives. That gives even more reason why every Christian should vote. The ballot is part of our great American heritage and freedom. It is our only means of keeping government clean and proper. I think that it is not only the right, but the duty of every American to use his franchise, prayerfully and thoughtfully.

Russia is an example of a country which was indifferent to corrupt politics, and when the Communists took over, they destroyed the partisan system, and, subsequently, the right of free franchise. Let us hope that the indifference of our people toward the importance of voting will not lead to a similar situation in the years to come.

In the last war my husband was killed by the Nazi troops. I have not been able to overcome my hatred for Germans since then and I resent the financial aid we give them. What is the answer to such a problem?

First you must recognize that there is a difference between troop actions in wartime and personal actions in peacetime. Back of German military operations was a machine that must be held responsible. There are some wonderful people among the Germans and we must not allow such feeling to jeopardize a possible friendship with a great nation. Second, there is the more personal problem of hatred that is directly related to a lack of spiritual adjustment. In our times we are constantly reminded of maladjusted people but we seldom hear of a maladjustment to God. This is what lies at the base of all hatred, jealousy, envy, deceit, and passion. I think you have both an intellectual and a spiritual problem. If you treat them both and settle each on its own merit, you will find that you will have a genuine respect and love for this people. They have given to the world some of its great leaders in religion, technology, and politics. Let us have a sympathetic understanding that will bring about co-operation. Let us also be certain of our proper relationship to God through an active faith in Christ.

I live in the suburb of a Northern city. A Negro family bought a house in our area. This has created a great deal of discussion, and tension. Having spent several winters on the Mississippi Gulf Coast, I find there is as much racial prejudice in the North as there is in the South. What can we Christians do about it?

I think Christ was quite definite as to the position that every true Christian should take. He said: "Thou shalt love thy neighbor as thyself." We must approach our racial problems with love, tolerance, and a spirit of give and take, no matter what the conditions. There is no excuse for any Christian to participate in acts of violence against a person because of race. The Scripture says in Proverbs 10:12: "Hatred stirreth up strifes, but love covereth all sins." Again the Scripture says in I John 2:9: "He that saith he is in the light, and hateth his brother is in darkness even until now." A true Christian will have love, tenderness, compassion, and understanding when he approaches this problem that threatens to divide the country.

Do you think the church ought to concern itself with politics, or should it confine itself entirely to a spiritual ministry?

This is one of those questions to which the answer is: It all depends on what you mean by a word. Here, of course, the critical word is the word "politics."

If we use the word to denote what is usually called party politics, then clearly the church ought not to interfere in such matters. It is not the business of the church to judge the merits of rival systems or programs of government—unless any such system or program flagrantly disregards God's commandments. Still less is it the church's business to identify itself with any one political party, as though that were the only "Christian" party.

But the word politics has a much wider and worthier meaning than that which we have so far attached to it. It really has reference to the community life of a town or city —and with this, needless to say, Christianity is very deeply concerned.

Christianity is a personal and also a social religion. Part of its "spiritual ministry" is to bring men into a right relationship with one another as well as with God. And the church is not preaching the whole Gospel unless it emphasizes social righteousness in addition to proclaiming personal salvation.

The common life of humanity is part of the church's concern because it is part of God's concern; and in these days, especially, it is important that men should be reminded that *all* life—political, social, economic, and industrial—must be subject to the eternal laws of God.

Don't you think the Christian church should take a more aggressive and positive stand with respect to the great problems of our day, such as the outlawing of the atomic bomb experiments?

The church has a very specific assignment, and that assignment is to teach the Gospel to every creature. I do not believe that a clear-thinking Christian is in favor of the advancement of the use of weapons that can annihilate the human race. In fact, the Christian church is committed to the propagation of peace. However, we must be careful not to impose Christian ethics and principles on people who have never yielded to the Gospel message. Although they are bound to feel the impact of the conversion of multitudes of people, yet society itself can never be renovated and renewed until every individual comes under the influence of the Gospel of Christ. You can be sure that if this took place that no use would be made of these terrible weapons of destruction. As it is, we can only hope that wicked men will refrain from the use of such weapons and give us the blessing and privilege of a world that is at peace.

As long as there are gangsters in a community there is need for a police force. Unfortunately, there are also international gangsters.

The peace Christ promised was actually individual peace. He indicated that "international peace" would come only when He had set up His kingdom.

Why don't you preachers talk more about social reforms? It seems to me that you are floating around on a cloud, when you ought to get down to earth and help solve the big problems of the day.

Jesus was one of the greatest social reformers, but He accomplished it by transforming the individual. He was not a revolutionist, He was the Redeemer; but by redeeming the individual personality, He brought about many social reforms. The abolition of slavery, the dignity of womanhood, our modern system of civil justice, and many other gains in human progress can be traced to Christian influence.

When our thinking is wrong concerning God, our thinking becomes warped about our fellow men. We believe that the best way to improve the social order is to improve the nature of man through the redemption of Christ.

Lyman Abbott was a famous preacher and advocate of social reform at the close of the last century. In his letter of resignation as pastor of Plymouth Congregational Church, Brooklyn, in 1899 he said: "I see that what I had once hoped might be done for my fellows through schemes of social reform and philanthropy can only be done by the influence of Jesus Christ. There is no dynamo in reform save the Cross of Jesus Christ."

Chapter 18

Christianity and Communism

Everyone today fears Communism. Do you think that Communism will ultimately destroy the Christian faith?

I do not believe that Communism will be able to destroy the true Christian faith. What it may do is to destroy a kind of pseudo-Christianity which lacks the inward conviction and vitality of a supernatural faith.

Christianity is a supernatural religion. It rests upon a supernatural faith. It was born and grew to maturity in the Roman world which was pagan and opposed to Christianity. It has never needed the sponsorship of any government in order to thrive. Jesus once said: "Upon this rock will I build my church and the gates of hell shall not prevail against it."

Christians may be called upon to suffer for their faith as the early martyrs did. But that does not mean that Christianity will be destroyed. The problem today is that too many professing Christians fear any persecution or suffering for the cause of Christ. But fear not, for if and when the time for suffering comes, God will supply an abundance of courage and strength for the ordeal.

In Acts, Chapter 4 we see the disciples selling all and putting their money in a common treasury, and all sharing alike. What is the difference between this and the Communistic belief?

There is a great difference here. The "having all things common" of the early Christians was based entirely on love. There was no force or coercion. There were no police to enforce the will of authorities. In fact there were no authorities; it was entirely a matter of the heart.

At this time in Jerusalem there was much poverty and the disciples were just fresh from being filled with the Holy Spirit. They felt an inner compulsion to share with others; they were full of the new Gospel "Love thy neighbor as thyself," and it spilled over into their social life.

If we spent more time with the Lord and were filled with the Holy Spirit, we too would be compelled to share both our goods and our faith with others. We would not only give of our means, but of our goods, our time, and our talents that others might discover the joy we know.

How do you explain the statement of Jesus, "Blessed are the meek for they shall inherit the earth," when it seems that Communism is the movement that seems most likely to do so? Certainly they do not exemplify meekness, do they? Or are some of these Scriptures not to be taken literally?

Jesus was always speaking of the final outcome. In history, many times it has appeared that righteousness didn't pay while expediency did. Men without principle often have their day of prosperity. The reason many people are puzzled about certain statements in the Bible is that they forget that the message of the Bible is given in terms of the final outcome. Each of the Beatitudes promises "blessedness" or the highest happiness to those who live according to its standards.

You must remember that God speaks in terms of the eternal. Happiness is not a fleeting thing but something that God intends will be our eternal condition. In an hour of darkness such as the present one, we submit to God, knowing that the outcome will be according to His promise no matter how discouraging the present moment may be. Peter once said: "But, beloved, be not ignorant of this one thing, that one day is with the Lord as a thousand years, and a thousand years as one day" (II Peter 3:8).

In an hour when it appears as if Russia might dominate us, can we not rely on the fact that this nation is better than Russia, and therefore God will not allow that wicked nation to overcome a good one?

I wish I could have such confidence, but unhappily it is not according to God's pattern nor His word. Many good nations have been overrun by those more wicked. That is because there are so many hidden elements involved in judgment. We can only see the surface appearance.

But you have also raised a question concerning goodness. Are we really a good people? If taking the lead among the nations for crime is goodness and if exalting the sensuous is goodness, then we are. But if these are otherwise, then we may be lagging in basic integrity and morality.

Even if we are better than some other nations, God might still chasten us under the hand of another nation to bring us back to a place of fearing Him and loving Him.

One of the prophets complained, "For the wicked doth compass about the righteous; therefore wrong judgment proceedeth" (Habakkuk 1:4). But God corrected his error and told him that "I am working a work in your day, which ye will not believe though it be told you." In an age such as this one, the people of God were counseled to live by faith, and not to judge by appearance of the moment. That is what we must do in ours.

Chapter 19

When You Face the Sunset Years

I am seventy-two years old. I have a depressed and hopeless feeling. I have no living relatives. Is there anything left in life for a man of my age? If so, how can I find it?

A very old man—much older than you—when he lay dying, said, "I have found that all the sugar is at the bottom of the cup." Life can grow sweeter and more rewarding as we grow older if we possess the presence of Christ. Bifocals and gray hair are no barriers to rich adventure. There can be no depression and no loneliness if Christ is centered in your life. Sunsets are always glorious. It is Christ who adds colors, glory, and beauty to man's sunsets. Try to find one person a day to whom you can add your new joy in Christ.

I am a doctor who has given his life to a community for many years for small fees. Now that I am old, I have no security and no support. This has created a bitter and resentful feeling in me toward those I have served. Is there an answer to such a bitter spirit?

It is one of the common experiences of life that old people so frequently become bitter and resentful. When one has given generously of his time and effort for the good of others, it is natural when that generosity is not returned for that person to resent the ungratefulness of the masses. Your natural

171

goodness and generosity are not always returned as you expect. Unless there is another motive for service, one cannot help becoming bitter. If your service is given in the name of Christ then you can serve without hoping for reward. Jesus gave Himself to and for sinning humanity and His giving was prompted by love. Even now, there is a chance for you, for if you would even at this late date in your life surrender your life to Christ and receive Him as Saviour and Lord, you would have the inward sweetness and love that are a byproduct of a changed life.

Another point, it seems to me that your community has a responsibility to you that they are neglecting. The neglect of older people is becoming an increasing sin in America.

I am a very old man now. I have been very wicked all my life. Just recently I found Jesus through one of your radio broadcasts. Is there any way I can redeem the years I have lost?

Sin makes an indelible impression on us in this life. You will never get over the regret of having lived for the devil all these years. But God can do the impossible. God can do more with a few days of your time if given completely to Him than He can with a whole life that is characterized by a halfhearted service. The lukewarm Christian can accomplish nothing with a whole life in which to do it. If you have lived for sin and self these many years, your witness will have telling effect on all who have known you. They will see the change and will be deeply impressed by God's power in your life. In your short time, take advantage to let everyone know the change that has been wrought in you through your faith in Christ. God can, through your yieldedness, accomplish much in a short time. Now is not the time for discouragement, but for a song of triumph and victory. Let everyone know of God's grace toward you.

I am a very old man. All my life I have been a churchgoer, and have lived an honest and decent life. In your preaching notice that you speak so often of joy and peace. I have never known any joy, and have often longed for peace but have found none. Is this a matter of personality and temperament, or have I just missed something?

It has been thought by many that to be religious is to be serious and even gloomy. Jesus did not teach it this way. He said: "Peace I leave with you, My peace I give unto you." The Psalmist said: "In thy presence is fullness of joy," and Paul said: "Rejoice in the Lord and again I say Rejoice." These are not the sayings of advocates of a gloomy and desolate religion. Christianity gives men and women a song and a smile, no matter what the circumstances are.

It may be that you have never had more than just "religion." Unless you have discovered the glorious person of Christ, and unless you have been drawn to Him, you have no genuine cause for joy. Sin has taken the joy out of the lives of many, and only the forgiveness of sins can restore that joy. Sin has robbed men of the inward abiding peace we all seek, and only the Saviour can give it. But also a religion apart from the experience of a risen Christ can leave you miserable. Let go of "religion" and lay hold of the person of Christ by faith and these things will be yours. Old age need not be a time of sorrow but increasing joy.

A friend of mine recently lost her husband. Although she has been a fine Christian, she seems to have lost interest in everything. What help or counsel should I give her?

The husband-wife relationship is the closest of all earthly relationships, and it is not to be wondered at that the death of one will come as a blow to the other. It does not mean that the bereaved is without faith in God or deficient in faith. The Bible teaches that on the occasion of death "we sorrow" (I Thessalonians 4:13). Abraham, who is cited as an example of faith, wept and sorrowed at the death of his wife, Sarah (Genesis 23:2). But the Christian does not sorrow as do those who are without hope. He looks forward to the time of the resurrection and reunion. Point out these wonderful truths to your bereaved friend, and pray for her that the Lord will use His Word to afford her comfort in a time of deep sorrow and loss. Show her that the loss is her loved one's gain, and at worst is only temporary.

I am a very old man and have been very wicked all my life. I would like to turn to God now but am afraid He won't accept me at this late hour. Besides, I am no longer able to do anything to merit His favor. Can you help me?

Don't you know that the desire to know the Lord shows that the Spirit of God is now speaking to you, otherwise you would have no desire? Your age is not the most important consideration in this matter so long as there is the desire. Jesus once gave a parable to show that it makes no difference providing you respond to the invitation when it is given. That parable is found in Matthew 20:1–16 and ends with the familiar verse: "So the last shall be first and the first last."

There is a good reason why this is so. Salvation does not depend on your personal merit but on the merit of Jesus Christ. In a lifetime you could not store up sufficient merit to enter Heaven. Concerning this Paul once wrote: "Where is the glorying? It is excluded. By what manner of law? Of works? Nay, but by a law of faith." I urge you, then, to respond to the urge to trust Christ, for He is able to save all that come unto God by Him.

I have passed the proverbial "three score years and ten," have been pensioned by my company, and in general seem quite useless. Actually, I feel very well and would like to be doing things, but nobody wants my help.

You can have some of your most useful and happy years before you. With no responsibilities in employment you can devote your time, strength, and wisdom gained from experience to help in very worthwhile projects in your church and community. Your busy pastor has many little tasks that are really important in themselves which he can assign to you. There are shut-ins to visit and widows and orphans to advise, the discouraged to cheer, the young men to counsel. With an old head and a young heart you can be a source of real strength to the many who need your cheer and encouragement. In your community you will find tasks that should be done, but are overlooked or neglected by busy people in the prime of life, and which you can do very satisfactorily. If you seem to be "on the shelf" make sure that you are on a shelf so low that your friends and neighbors can reach you easily and enlist you to help them do the things for which you are much better qualified than they. Just do not sit in the corner and look inwardly; rather, be on the corner to respond to the challenge—and above all make sure you have made preparation for the inevitable by accepting Christ as your personal Lord and Saviour. Life does not begin at forty but with God.

I went to church as long as I could. Now I am elderly and infirm and cannot attend services. Does this really matter? I try to live a Christian life and do all the good I can for others.

I am glad to take this opportunity of sending a brief message to you and other shut-in Christians who are denied the privilege of worshiping in church on Sundays.

Such worship is, I know, one of the great joys of the Christian life and a real means of grace, but I would ask you to remember that true worship is not dependent upon particular times and places.

Read in your Bible what the Lord Jesus said about that to the Samaritan woman (John 4:19–24).

Your home may be your Bethel where you find God's presence always near and in the sanctuary of your heart you may draw near to Him at all times through Jesus Christ.

Participate when you can in the religious services on the radio. This will give you a sense of fellowship with other Christians and help you to feel that you are not entirely cut off from the worship of the church.

Above all, I would urge you to exercise a special ministry of prayer during these days. Make this a real piece of Christian service as you remember before God the needs of His church and His world.

Chapter 20

What About Death . . . and Beyond?

I am afraid to die. I have tried to get over this fear, but cannot. Is there anything one can do to overcome it?

The fear of death is a condition that is perfectly normal for any who have never come to Christ. Death is an experience from which we shrink, yet for the Christian, the fear is removed. He has the assurance that the sins for which he would be judged at death have been dealt with, whereas the non-Christian has no such assurance.

Many non-Christians try to convince themselves that they do not believe in the supernatural, nor in a hereafter. Try as they will, there lingers the deep consciousness that we have not been created for time alone. We instinctively know that justice alone demands some judgment day. Unless we have knowingly settled the question of our sinfulness, we have this fear. Until you acknowledge this basic truth, your fears will continue. If you would admit the possibility of the supernatural and acknowledge the facts of the Gospel as they apply to your own life, you would find the fear of death removed and the glorious peace of believing a part of your life.

Last night I dreamed I was dying and woke up in an agony of fear. Today I know I am not ready to die. What must I do?

God may have permitted you to have this dream to make you realize that you have neglected the most important thing in this life and in the next. You can have peace in your heart and the assurance of salvation if you will humbly acknowledge yourself as a sinner in God's sight, ask His forgiveness and cleaning and trust in Jesus Christ, God's Son, as your Saviour from sin. Christ died on the Cross to do just this very thing for you. Let me urge you to get a Bible and read, or ask someone to help you read the following verses: Romans 3:12, Romans 3:23, II Timothy 3:5, Romans 3:19, Ephesians 2:8, Luke 19:10, Romans 5:8, Hebrews 7:25, Romans 10:13, and Romans 10:9, 10. These are not magic verses. They simply tell us about our need and how to find that need met in Jesus Christ. You do not have to do some wonderful thing to be saved. All you have to do is accept the wonderful thing Christ has done for you. After you have this assurance in your heart tell other people about it. Also, show by your daily life that Christ has changed it for His own glory.

I am a nurse working in a large city hospital. I love the work and get real satisfaction out of meeting the needs of those who are suffering. I also believe I have been able to bring cheer to those who are lonely. When I have to witness the death of some people, I am stricken with fear. That is the only time I don't like the work. Someone told me it was a spiritual problem, but I don't know. What do you think?

The fear of death is something that all people have sometime. With many, this fear is greatly aggravated. You did not tell me if you were a believer in Christ or not, for that makes a great difference. Christ has removed forever the fear of death for those who believe in Him. He has brought life and immortality to light through the Gospel. Man, by nature, fears death because death is always associated with judgment and with the unknown. We fear it because we do not know what lies ahead. But Christ has made the way for us through His own death. He provides eternal life and has promised His presence in all of life's experiences, and even in death. "Yea, though I walk through the valley of the shadow of death I will fear no evil," said the Psalmist. You, too, can lose that fear when you commit your whole self to Christ, trust Him for salvation from sin, and He will remove the sting of death, which is sin.

I cannot get over a childhood fear. Frankly, I'm afraid to die, and when I went to a minister to receive help, he did his best to convince me that such fears can be overcome by saying that death will be a glorious adventure. Isn't that just what the Bible teaches?

No, not quite. Death will be a wonderful and glorious adventure for those who are prepared for it, but not for all. The fear of death is a fear that many have, but they manage to quiet their fear by refusing to think or speak about it. But, sadly, they never solve the problem by refusing to discuss it or think upon it. The Bible clearly warns us to "Prepare to meet thy God" and that means to meet Him in judgment. It is because one is not prepared that he has fears. The Bible says that "the sting of death is sin," and until we settle the sin problem, death remains something to be rightly feared. The Bible answer to that fear is to repent of sin and receive Christ as Saviour and Lord. With the sin problem settled, death will have no sting and most of its fears will be gone.

I have been in the Protestant branch of the church for many years. Now as I am growing older and facing the end, as we must all do, I fear that I am not ready spiritually. Is that because I haven't been faithful to my church? What can I do now that I am old?

At some time you got the notion that your church would secure your spiritual condition and ready you for heaven. You have made a very crucial mistake in this matter. The church does have a most important function in its proclamation of the Gospel message to the world and its instruction to believers. But important as this ministry is, it can only make the all-important announcement. The individual must himself become related to God through faith in Christ.

Many people confuse corporeal membership with spiritual

membership in the church. Their names are written in the church roll, but they have never appropriated salvation through trust in Christ. Herein is your hope now. You can still make that decision and come to the end of your days with a deep inward peace. Jesus once said, "Him that cometh unto me I will in no wise cast out." Like the thief on the cross, you too can come, but I urge you not to delay a single day. Tomorrow may be too late.

I have a terrible fear of death. I am getting old and this fear haunts me by night and by day. Is this evidence that I am not a Christian? I have always thought that I was.

Let me begin by saying that everyone, including most devout people, has some fear about departing this life. It is human to dread the unknown, and death is a mysterious journey. But I do not believe that the true believer should cringe before, and be cowed by, the thought of death. Christ threw a radiant rainbow of hope around the grave when He said: "He that believeth in me, though he were dead, yet shall he live." Christian faith is one which goes down into the grave with the firm confidence that Christ took the sting and stigma out of death. As Paul said when he faced the Last Enemy: "O death, where is thy sting: O grave, where is thy victory?"

Longfellow said: "The grave itself is but a covered bridge, leading from light to light, through a brief darkness!"

On the grave of Henry Alford, who wrote the hymn "Ten Thousand Times Ten Thousand" are these words: "The inn of a pilgrim journeying to Jerusalem."

You should make sure about your personal relationship to Christ. Remember David said: "Yea though I walk through the valley of the shadow of Death, I will fear no evil, for Thou art with me." Make sure Christ is with you and you will not fear.

I've always believed in God, but since our precious baby lived only a week, I'm despondent. I can't seem to pray any more. How can I find courage to go on?

I wish I could sit down and talk to you, and give a full hour to answering your question. A situation like yours puts Christianity to the supreme test. Don't imagine that you are the only one who has had moments of spiritual blindness. Even the saints had their dark days. But they found God again. You can, too. Do these four things:

1. Each morning kneel and thank God for all the joy He has brought through the years. Surrender your day to Him. Ask Christ to guide and direct you. Then all through the day think of Him as walking by your side.

2. Read your Bible. There you will find words of wisdom and comfort, as "For now we see through a glass, darkly; but then face to face: now I know in part; but then shall I know even as also I am known" (I Corinthians 13:12).

3. Seek opportunities to help those in need. There is someone who needs your love and care. Ask God to show you who it is.

4. Hold fast to your belief in Eternal Life. Death is not the end, but the doorway into heaven.

This is a difficult hour for you. Remember that Jesus did not promise that His followers would escape suffering and heartache. No, He promised instead that they would have peace in the midst of pain, and be given a divine strength to support them in hours of weakness. The Bible says: "This is the victory that overcometh the world, even our faith" (I John 5:4).

Recently my aged mother died, and instead of a conventional burial I had her cremated. I would have respected her wishes but she never indicated any preference. Recently someone told me that it was contrary to the teaching of the Bible, because it destroyed the body which God would raise up at the last day. Was I un-Christian in doing this thing?

It is true that cremation is of pagan tradition, but that does not necessarily make it a sinful act. As an alternative to burial, it has been generally accepted by many people, both Christian and non-Christian. I am confident that it has nothing whatever to do with the resurrection of the body. Many Christians have been accidentally burned, some were burned as martyrs, but this certainly will not limit God in the resurrection.

The Bible teaches that we will have a new body in the resurrection. The Bible says: "But God giveth it a body even as it pleased Him, and to each seed a body of its own" (I Corinthians 15:38).

It appears that the actual mode of disposing of the dead is not the crucial issue and it need cause you no remorse. If your mother had her personal faith in Christ, she then met the only condition for sharing in the glorious resurrection of the just. That is why the Christian can assuredly say that the grave is not the end.

Recently a very close friend of mine, one whom I love dearly, died and left me behind. What I am concerned about now is whether or not we forget our loved ones after death. Has my friend forgotten me? Does she know anything about me? When I die will I remember the people whom I leave behind?

Frankly, the Bible is silent concerning this matter. It does not tell whether those who have gone to be with the Lord, or whether those who are dead without Christ are able to remember anything about their loved ones. There is at least one scripture that indicates that the unconverted will remember the condition of their unconverted friends. This story Jesus tells in Luke 16:19–31. He describes a man who is dead and in hell as looking up and pleading for his brothers whom he knows are unconverted. Read this tragic story and you will see. On the other hand we are given to believe that those who have died and gone to be with the Lord are free from any kind of earthly anxiety. If they are able to remember their loved ones, it is only because those loved ones have already committed their lives into the care and keeping of a loving Saviour. God is merciful and permits those who are dead in Christ to forget all of those things that would diminish their joy.

There are many good reasons for being a Christian. In this life one has the presence and comfort of God's presence throughout all of the trials that come to us in our daily activities. Then, when it comes to the matter of facing eternity, we have the added comfort of knowing that all of our sins have been forgiven and Christ is ready to receive us. Philippians 1:23 clearly describes the fact that "to depart and to be with Christ is very far better."

Many people want to live more than anything else. The Christian who wants to live has a definite object. He wants to live to serve Christ, but he neither fears death nor tries to avoid it because he knows that to be dead and to be in the presence of Christ is the greatest reward one can have.

Can a man live in sin all his life and yet have God save his soul at the time he dies?

One's salvation is not determined by the time of life at which we repent and accept Christ as our Saviour. There have been those who have repented on their deathbeds and have been saved. In the Bible we have the incident where one of the thieves crucified with Jesus turned to Christ in repentance and was told, "This day shalt thou be with me in paradise." However, for one to deliberately wait until near the end of life is to take a desperately dangerous course. None of us knows when we may die; for thousands, sudden death occurs each day. But more important even than the foolishness of deliberately waiting is the fact that every day we delay we are losing the joy of being a Christian and also losing the opportunity to witness and live for Christ. There are some who think of being a Christian as something lacking in joy. As a matter of fact, the only people in the world who have any right to be happy are Christians, as they know where they are now and where they are going. The Bible says: "Behold, now is the accepted time; behold, now is the day of salvation." While there is always hope for the repentant sinner, the longer one waits to accept Christ the more difficult it becomes. His grace is always ready and willing but the heart of man grows harder all the time.

Recently, some friends and I were discussing whether we go immediately to Heaven when we die. Can you help us with the answer to this question?

The Bible clearly teaches that when a believer in Christ dies, he goes to be with the Lord. "Absent from the body, at home with the Lord" is what Paul said about it (II Corinthians 5:8). Also, in one of Jesus' parables he told of the rich man and Lazarus who were already at their destination. But the Bible also teaches that there is a day of resurrection and judgment which is yet future (II Timothy 2:18). Here reference to a past resurrection is misleading and in error. It is the coming event when Jesus comes again. The Bible says: "For if we believe that Jesus died and rose again, even so them also that are fallen asleep in Jesus will God bring with Him . . . For the dead in Christ shall rise first, then we that are alive and remain shall be caught up together with them to meet the Lord" (I Thessalonians 4:14, 17). The answer seems to be that there is an intermediate state when we are with the Lord, but have not yet received the glorious body of the resurrection.

If we are fortunate enough to go to heaven, will we know our loved ones there? Would you tell me the Scripture for this?

We have no reason to believe that we shall be less intelligent in Heaven than we are upon earth. The Bible says: "Now we see through a glass darkly; but then face to face; now I know in part; but then shall I know even also as I am known" (I Corinthians 13:12).

But if your question suggests that we will see our loved ones in the same light as we see them upon this earth, I will have to say that we will not. While the family is a sacred institution, and much in the Bible is addressed to family love, family responsibility, and family loyalty, "when that which is perfect is come, then that which is in part shall be done away." God instituted family life for a twofold purpose: the propagation of the race, and Divine instruction. In the resurrection, Christ said, "They neither marry, nor are given in marriage, but are as the angels of God in Heaven."

We will know our loved ones in Heaven, of course, and will remember them, even as the rich man in hell remembered his brothers. But we will find fellowship with all members of the family of the redeemed, and not just with our flesh and blood. "When that which is perfect is come, that which is in part, will be done away."

It is difficult to rationalize on the unknown. We can but cite Scriptures related to the subject. This we do know: "Eye hath not seen, nor ear heard . . . what God has prepared for those who love Him."

Will we be in body and spirit in heaven or just in spirit? I believe the Bible says that we will have a new body. If so, where is the reference in the Bible?

Our finite minds cannot fully perceive all of the mysteries of the future life. The Bible does say: "We look for the Saviour, the Lord Jesus Christ, who *shall change our vile body, that it may be fashioned like unto His glorious body . . .*" (Philippians 3:21).

After the resurrection, Jesus appeared in a glorified, heavenly body. He ate, talked, and was capable of being felt, as in the case of Thomas who felt His wounds and said: "My Lord and my God." But this body was indestructible, it passed through stone walls, and finally ascended into heaven. There is every indication in the Bible that Christians will be clothed in immortality, even as was Christ. Paul said: "For this corruptible must put on incorruption, and this mortal shall put on immortality." Our earthly bodies are fairly well suited to conditions of our earthly existence, but the Bible says that these bodies must undergo a transformation to fit them for heavenly conditions. This promise of a glorified body is given only to those who have trusted Christ for salvation. Heaven is a quality and state of life given only to the redeemed.

After a person has died and gone to another life, does he know or realize what he did while on this earth?

While it is not given us to know all of the details about the afterlife, we are given some insights into some aspects of it.

In the parable of the rich man and Lazarus, Christ indicated that the rich man could recall many of the events of earth. Particularly did he remember the sins of omission. He remembered that he had ignored the need of the beggar Lazarus. He remembered his five brothers and feared that they might also end up in hell, and asked that a messenger might be sent to earth to warn them.

There are evidences that we will remember many of the events of life. In the light of eternity, we will see that the things we thought so important were unimportant, and that the things we considered unimportant were really the things we should have attended to. Part of hell's torments will be the suffering of remorse, and of regretful memory.

For the saved, there will be the joys of having been faithful, and the thrill of unfolding knowledge throughout eternity. The Bible says: "Now we see through a glass darkly; but then face to face; now I know in part; but then shall I know even also as I am known" (I Corinthians 13:12).

In the afterlife, will a man and woman who have been married remain married? When a person dies, will he remain the same age throughout eternity?

The marriage contract terminates at death. "Until death do us part" is the clause we repeat when we are wed. Legally, and in the sight of God, all marriages are dissolved when one or the other of the partners enters eternity.

The Sadducees asked Jesus this same question and He said: "The children of this world marry and are given in marriage: but they which shall be accounted worthy to obtain that world, and the resurrection from the dead, neither marry, nor are given in marriage" (Luke 20:34–35).

Yet I am certain that in heaven everything will be there needful for our complete happiness. I am equally certain that married couples will know and love each other in the afterlife—though the relationship will be no longer physical but spiritual.

As to remaining the same age throughout eternity, heaven has no clocks nor calendars, and "time will be no more." The thing with which we should be most concerned is preparing for eternity, and though we may find the answer to every mystery, but fail to prepare to meet God, we will be in hopeless straits in the world to come.

What is your opinion with regard to the soul after death? Does it lie in the grave until the resurrection or does it go straight to God?

It is unwise to speculate beyond those things clearly stated in the Bible. To the repentant thief on the cross, Jesus said: "Today shalt thou be with me in paradise." This would indicate that the soul of a Christian at death goes immediately to be with the Lord in glory. At the same time, that is not the final state of the believer for at the resurrection, the bodies and souls of believers will be reunited and we will be given a glorified body which will live forever in God's presence. In the first book of Thessalonians we are told: "For the Lord Himself shall descend from heaven with a shout, with the voice of the archangel, and with the trump of God; and the dead in Christ shall rise first: then we which are alive and remain shall be caught up together with them in the clouds, to meet the Lord in the air: and so shall we ever be with the Lord." There are many mysteries which have been withheld from our knowledge. But this we can affirm: the person who puts his trust in Jesus Christ and what He has done for us is immediately changed from death to life; he has been born again and physical death can never separate him from God. If you believe in Christ, you have eternal life now and death is but a transition into His presence.

Chapter 21

"I Wonder About Salvation"

I don't agree with you when you make such general statements about everybody being a sinner. There are many wonderful people in the world who certainly don't belong in the hoodlum and criminal class.

You have not asked me a question, but I can tell you why I have repeated the assertion that all have sinned. There are basically two reasons why I insist upon this. First, the Bible says so: "All have sinned and come short of the glory of God." If there were no other reason, that in itself would be sufficient. But there is a second reason also. Human nature is best explained when you accept this view. The wonderful and good people you mention are without doubt as good as you say when judged by human standards. It is when we make the comparison with the holiness of God that we realize the truth of this statement. Any person that is not fully as good as Jesus Christ is a sinner. He alone is the world's only example of one who was without sin. Every other person, even the good and wonderful ones you may have in mind, have their weak moments when they fall below their own faulty standards. That is why we all need a sinless Saviour. Of Jesus, the Bible says: "He who knew no sin, was made to be sin on our behalf that we might be made the righteousness of God in Him" (II Corinthians 5:21).

188

I have recently started my college studies, and among my first subjects I am studying the psychology of religion. My professor tells me that conversion is nothing more than a psychological phenomenon experienced by most religions. Right now I am plenty worried about the things I learned in my home church, for they seem to be slipping away from me. Do you think my conversion was real?

Certainly your conversion was real, if when you were converted you came from darkness to the light of the Gospel. If you received Jesus Christ as your Lord and Saviour, then and there you became a new creature. I wouldn't take anything for granted, not even a religious experience. You see, your professor is right when he says there are conversions experienced in most religions. But don't allow that to disturb you, for though all men may have some kind of a religious experience, only the ones who receive Jesus Christ in a moment of repentance and faith are born again. The fact that others have similar religious emotions and conversions merely shows that God so made man that he is capable of being converted. How tragic it is when a man is converted falsely! I'll tell you what to do. To overcome your fears and intellectual dilemma, just give as much time to the study of what God has to say about it as your professor does. Don't argue with him, but test everything he says in the light of God's word. You need have no fear then, for the Bible can stand the onslaught of the enemy.

I want to be a Christian and live for the Lord. I believe in the Lord Jesus Christ with all my heart and pray, but I don't feel any change in myself. What can I do?

Your question expresses all the requirements for being a Christian. You say you want to be a Christian—you have desire. You believe with all your heart—you have faith. And you have prayed—that is communication. But you add that you don't feel any change. It could be that you are expecting some earth-shaking emotion and that is where you are making a mistake. You may not feel any change, but the fact that you hunger for God, that you believe, and that you pray, all signify that there is a change in your life.

For the sake of illustration, let us say that you owed a bill that you were unable to pay, and a friend with adequate resources paid that bill for you. For further proof that the debt was canceled, let us say that you received a statement from your creditor informing you that the bill was paid in full. You would be foolish to go around saying that you just couldn't believe the debt was paid, and that you didn't feel any different.

The cross of Christ cancels your sins for the Bible says so. "And having made peace through the blood of His cross, by Him to reconcile all things to Himself." You have accepted God's estimate of your sins, and now you must accept God's estimate of Christ's redemptive work on the Cross. Not only believe it, but accept it, and live by it.

I was reared in a Christian home where the Bible was clearly taught and believed. Since I have grown up I have seen older people converted and how they rejoiced. I have never had this kind of feeling. Is it because I have been taught about Jesus and "good" all my life?

There are perhaps two reasons why you have never experienced this "joy" you have observed in other people.

First, if you accepted Christ in early life, the transition from innocent childhood to a believing Christian was not nearly so noticeable as it is in a mature person whose conscience has been weighed down with years of accumulated guilt. To illustrate: let us say that a farmer and his son were walking home from the cornfield. The boy carries a few ears in his hands, but the father bends beneath the weight of a hundred-pound sack of corn. Now, suppose a friend comes down that road with a wagon and offers to carry father and son home. He carries the load of each, but it is obvious that the father would be the more relieved and grateful of the two. The child coming to Christ, because his burden of sin is light, may not experience the overwhelming joy of the confirmed sinner who finds relief from his guilt through Christ. His load was greater—thus his joy is greater.

The other reason could well be that you have trusted in your good upbringing rather than in the person of Christ. Only you can decide which applies to your case.

I have broken about every one of the Ten Commandments in the Bible. I am really sorry for my wrongdoing and am trying to live a Christian life. But somehow I wonder if God can really forgive all I have done. Is there some way I can really know where I stand with God?

There is no doubt about God's willingness to forgive you. The Bible is filled with such promises as: "I, even I, am He that blotteth out thy transgressions for mine own sake, *and will not remember thy sins.*"

There are two suggestions I would make to you. First, you say you are sorry for your sins. But there is a difference between remorse and repentance. Remorse means "being sorry for your sins," but repentance means "turning from your sins." Make sure you have turned from your sins. Don't just file them away for future reference, but put them out of sight and out of mind forever. The Bible says: "Let the wicked forsake his way, and the unrighteous man his thought, and let him return to the Lord, for *He will abundantly pardon.*" You must forsake before you are forgiven.

Second, it is possible that God has forgiven you but that you haven't forgiven yourself. If God loves you enough to forgive and forget the past, then you ought to forgive yourself. If a just God considers you forgiven, then you should forgive yourself.

I have confessed my past sins to God, but do I have to make public confession for the terrible sins committed in my younger days? There is no one living that is concerned in any way.

The confession of sin should be as public as was the deed. If you have wronged an individual, make amends to that individual. If you have sinned against a group, you must ask that group to forgive you. If you have sinned against your community, print your confession in the newspaper. That, I believe, is the Bible way. "If thou rememberest that thy brother hath aught against thee; . . . be reconciled to thy brother and then come and offer thy gift."

You say your sin concerns no living person. Then God, alone, should be your confessor. Confessing to other people may only complicate matters, and cast aspersions on your character. The Bible says: "If we confess our sins unto Him, He is faithful and just to forgive our sins and to cleanse us from all unrighteousness."

I cannot see how a sinner who has committed robbery, murder, and rape can go to God and ask forgiveness and get it.

This person you mention, to my way of thinking, certainly was in need of forgiveness! Is it your idea that only good people can be forgiven? The Bible says: "Christ came not to call the righteous, but sinners unto repentance."

The Pharisees didn't see how Jesus could forgive the adulteress, but He did! The wonderful thing about the grace of God is that it is particularly designed for sinners—bad sinners. Paul said: "Christ Jesus came into the world to save sinners, of whom I am chief." A person who feels smug about his goodness never makes a good disciple of Christ. You will remember the Pharisee and the Publican. The Pharisee said: "I thank thee Lord that I am not as other men." But the Publican said: "God be merciful to me a sinner!" The Bible says that the Publican went up to his house, justified—his attitude of repentance was pleasing to God, but the Pharisee's self-righteous attitude was repugnant to God.

Remember also the thief on the cross who said: "Lord, remember me." And Jesus said: "This day thou shalt be with me in paradise." God specializes in making sinners into saints!

Last night a bunch of us fellows got to discussing religion and the majority seemed to feel that if we do the best we can, we are Christians. If that is true, where does Christ come in?

Your discussion has really centered on the question whether a man can save himself; whether the best we may do is all that God requires of us. If man, by his own efforts, no matter how lofty and good they might be, is capable of saving himself, then there would have been no necessity for Christ to come into the world. The Bible says: "All have sinned and come short of the glory of God." The Bible also tells us that "the wages of sin is death." Man's big problem centers in the ugly little word "sin." We all are sinners by nature, by inheritance, and by practice. If we say we do not sin, we simply make God a liar. The next question naturally is whether we can do anything about our own sins. We may reform but we cannot change our hearts. It is no more possible for a man to redeem himself from the guilt and penalty of sin than it is for him to lift himself up by his boot straps. Then what can man do? Only one thing and that is to accept the provision God has made. This provision is in Jesus Christ, the Son of God, who came into this world for the express purpose of changing our sinful natures and giving us new hearts. This He does to all who in sincerity accept Him as their Saviour. This is the heart of the Gospel message and it is wonderful news.

My wife has always been a follower. Anything I suggest, she will go along with me. When I was living in sin, she took part in the sinful way of life. Recently I was converted, and now she goes with me to church and takes part in everything. How can I be sure she has also been converted?

Probably you can never be sure in your own mind if your wife is a true Christian if she is such a follower. You will have to be content to judge by the changed life. Even though she may have followed you in the sinful life, it is doubtful if she would do so when you have committed your life to Christ. Almost every time there is opposition from the unconverted partner to such a change. You should be very grateful to have a wife who does not oppose you in the new life you have begun.

Another thing you should know is that not every person is psychologically capable of experiencing conversion with the same radical effect as you did. Her mild disposition may mean that she would never have the revolutionary change you think she should. This does not mean that her conversion is less genuine or real. Just accept her confession and give thanks to God that you continue in such agreement.

How can a person know for sure if he is a Christian?

The Bible suggests ways in which we can have the assurance of our salvation.

We know because of a change that takes place. The Bible says: "Therefore if any man be in Christ, he is a new creature; old things are passed away; behold, all things are become new."

We know by the presence of God's Spirit in our lives. "Hereby we know that we dwell in Him, and He in us, because He hath given us of His Spirit."

We know we are Christian if love is the dominating force in our lives. "Beloved, let us love one another, for love is of God, and every one that loveth is born of God, and knoweth God . . . for God is love."

We know we are Christian when we find it in our hearts to obey God. "And hereby we do know that we know Him, if we keep His commandments."

And last but not least, we know because we receive Christ. "As many as received Him, to them gave He power to become the sons of God, even to them that believe on His name."

I have been studying Christianity, and have a question about some things I don't understand. How completely should one have answers to all of the problems before becoming a Christian?

Actually you will never find the answers until you do become a Christian. There are a host of spiritual problems that you cannot understand at all until you begin the Christian life. The reason is, those who have never exercised faith in Christ are called spiritually "blind," and therefore it is not possible to find answers. If you wait until you have a complete understanding of all the details of the Christian faith, then you will never be saved at all. Nicodemus, the teacher of Israel in the days of Jesus, once came to Jesus for the answer to some of his questions. Jesus did not answer a single question, but first pointed out that a man must be "born again" before he could "see spiritual truth." This takes place, not when you understand all things, but when you understand simply that you are sinful and in need of a Saviour, and that Jesus Christ is that Saviour you need. Forsake your sins and trust Him. Then the eyes of your mind will open to the glorious truths of God.

Do you think that people who are reared in a good Christian home need to come forward publicly and "accept Christ," as you say? Don't children who are raised in a Christian atmosphere just grow into the faith?

It is possible that children who are reared in a devout Christian home may have "accepted Christ" in the natural course of events without having a climactic, dramatic experience of conversion. My wife, Ruth, doesn't remember the exact moment that she accepted Christ, but there has never been a doubt that she has.

But, we must also remember that being reared in a Christian home will not, in itself, save one. As I have said, you may have been born in a garage, but that doesn't make you an automobile. The Christian faith is a personal thing. Notice the personal pronouns in this statement of St. Paul's: "I live by the faith of the Son of God who loved me, and gave Himself for me." There was no hearsay here, no harking back to a vague tradition. Our relationship to Christ is to be personal, vital, throbbing with reality. The Bible says: "By their fruits shall ye know them." If your life is producing the fruit of the Spirit, then that is convincing evidence that you have been born of the Spirit.

On the other hand, I know people who doubt their relationship to Christ. It is best for them to have an encounter with Christ in order to have "assurance."

It must be wonderful to have the comfort that your religion gives you. I only wish I had it, but common sense tells me better. Night after night in agony I suffer and call on God; and God has never yet said a word to this unbeliever.

If you truly call on God, then you are not "an unbeliever." However, if you are letting your "common sense" come between you and God, you are more than foolish. You may find that God has not answered you because you have closed your mind and heart to Him. Christ said: "God is a spirit and they that worship Him must worship Him in spirit and in truth." Again the Bible says: "But without faith it is impossible to please Him: For he that cometh to God must believe that He is, and that He is a rewarder of them that diligently seek Him." Have you exercised this faith? I doubt very much if you understand all of the processes of digestion and metabolism of food. But you probably eat regularly, with the full assurance that your food will nourish your body. Give God the same kind of chance. Accept Him by faith. Put your trust in Him and then you will have the glorious experience of realizing that He is everything to you. Forget about "common sense" and step out in faith. Christ's death on the Cross has been foolishness and a stumbling block to those who have rejected the salvation He offers in that way. But for all who will believe, it becomes the glorious power of God.

I am married to the nicest woman on earth and have two lovely children but I have defiled myself and other people by the rottenest kind of sins. My wife has recently sold her jewelry to pay my doctor's bill and I love her dearly but I don't know how to repay what I have done. I am dying of cancer and do not have more than six months to live. I don't hope to be saved because I know hell is too good for me. Any crumb of comfort will be appreciated.

My dear friend: You may be the blackest sinner who ever drew breath, and from the rest of your letter it is obvious that you have sunk in sin just about as far as possible. But I want to assure you on the promise of the Lord Jesus Christ Himself that if you will ask Him to forgive you and trust in Him as your Saviour you will surely be saved. Christ came into the world not to save good people but sinners. Those who think they are good are just fooling themselves. But when you admit your sinful life and realize there is nothing you can do, you are in the attitude of mind to let Christ take over. Take the Gospel of John and read it from beginning to end. Then read it again and again and take every promise and apply it to yourself. In John 6:37 you will find these words spoken by our Lord: ". . . and him that cometh to me I will in no wise cast out." This, along with many, many other promises, is given to us so that we can turn in faith and assurance and receive the cleansing and forgiveness Christ wants to give all of us. In Matthew 11:28, Christ says: "Come unto me, all ye that labour and are heavy laden, and I will give you rest." You are burdened down with a sense of sin and guilt, just turn it over to Jesus and He will completely remove it and give you a new heart and the joy of His presence in your heart.

Chapter 22

"I Wonder About Science and Outer Space"

In science class at school, all living things are classified as animals. Are human beings actually animals? Or does God classify them differently?

Biologically, man is an animal. That is to say, he does not make his own food by photosynthesis. He is thus distinguished from plant life. But he is more than an animal. He has three attributes which four-footed animals do not have: reason, conscience, and will. Animals are motivated by instinct. Their behavior patterns are instinctive, not intelligent. Since their responses are instinctive, they have no conscience. A dog probably feels no more remorse after biting a man than he does when chewing a bone. Then again, an animal's decisions are not volitional, but instinctive. He has no will, but acts instinctively, according to set, inner urges.

Why is man different than the other animals? Because he was created in the image of God. He was created with three attributes as we have said. The first man, Adam, used all three of these attributes. First, he reasoned that his own judgment was as good as God's, and he ate of the forbidden fruit. In that act, the will of man came into play, for he could have decided either way. Then, after he broke God's command, he felt conscience-stricken and ran away to hide in the garden. Strangely, this man-animal has been following that same pattern through the centuries. Within these God-given attributes are life or death, happiness or sorrow, and peace or conflict. If he dissipates the powers which God has given him, he is of all creatures most miserable. But if he uses them right, he can make of this world a paradise.

In my college class in advanced astronomy, the question has been raised whether the explosion theory of the origin of the universe permits the possibility of Divine creation. What do you think?

I do not feel competent to speak on the various theories held by scientists with reference to the origin of the universe. But this one thing I am very sure of—any theory which leaves the Sovereign God out of His own universe is a very poor one. For the creature to ignore the Creator is utter folly. To think that this universe, so vast that even now its limits are unknown, is the product of self-contained and self-directed matter seems hardly worthy of consideration. In our own world there are evidences on every hand that in all of nature there is a perfection and a controlling and directing hand which must be infinite and divine. Should we find a watch by the side of the road, and, should we never have seen a watch before, we would be led to believe in some being capable of thought and design who made that watch. How much more do we have evidence on every hand of God and of His creative power and wisdom. Psalm 19 tells us that the heavens and the earth show forth the glory of God. In the first chapter of Paul's letter to the Romans we read: "For the invisible things of him from the creation of the world are clearly seen, being understood by the things that are made." Any theory of the universe which does not take into account the God and Creator of that universe is not worthy of serious consideration.

I am a freshman in college and am greatly confused because we are being told that science has disproved much of the Bible and that I will have to "re-think" my faith if I expect to have any faith.

When you are told that science has disproved the Bible, ask specifically where such is the case. True science and a true understanding of the Bible are never at variance. Furthermore, at many points where it was thought a few years ago that science was disproving the Scripture, records have since been cleared up and the Bible is now admittedly correct. Of course, if one is definitely antagonistic to the Christian faith and the Scriptures, he is prone to back his position by supposed inaccuracies in the Bible. But the best answer to such people is to insist on a statement on their part of just what the inaccuracies are. In most cases they are not forthcoming. In others, if you do not have an explanation yourself you will be wise to ask your pastor or some Biblical scholar who can give you the answer. In truly scientific circles today there is much less antagonism to the Christian faith and to the Bible than was true a few years ago. This is due to the fact that scientific discoveries (not theories) are found more and more to fit into the record God has given us in His Word. Before you "re-think" your faith it may be wise to examine the critics of the Bible. In the end your faith will be even stronger.

What is your opinion of these rocket experiments? Will they interfere with the planets in any way, such as the power of the sun, or the disarrangement of the earth or moon? If so, can the Lord stop these adventures into space?

Though I am a minister and not a scientist, I have no qualms about the rocket experiments upsetting the order of the universe. It would be just as logical to get upset at children casting stones into the ocean, fearing that their childish actions might upside the rhythm of the tides. God's universe is so vast and limitless that man's probing into space is less expansive than a minute pinprick in the outer skin of an onion. Our solar system is just one of billions in God's colossal creation. No, I don't think you need to fear that the rocket experiments are endangering the universe.

Perhaps all this is to beckon our attention to the greatness and majesty of God. The Bible says: "When I consider thy heavens, the work of thy fingers, the moon and the stars, which thou hast ordained: What is man that thou art mindful of him? O Lord, how excellent is thy name in all the earth."

I am a student of the physical sciences. Some of my associates are inclined to believe that there is life on other planets. If there are people who inhabit these planets, what does that do to our faith in the Gospel? Can it be that God is primarily interested in this planet?

From my studies in the Scriptures I can find nothing that would change our essential faith in the Gospel if we did discover life on other planets. Our Bible is clearly designed for this particular planet with its particular problem of man's sin. When we observe this fact we are on safe ground. It is not a part of the Bible's message to inform us of what God has done elsewhere. Its message is concerned with earth dwellers, their origin, the reason for their existence, the cause of their misery and the plan of redemption for a fallen race. I am sure that if there are dwellers on other planets, they are either not involved in the sin problem, or else God has made satisfactory provision for them. The God of the Universe is the God of our Lord Jesus Christ. He is entirely able to support the entire creation and is able to govern it in righteousness.

Chapter 23

Matters Difficult to Understand

Some people say we should not take a critical attitude toward the Bible. How can one be intellectually honest and not do so? Are we to swallow the whole thing without examining it?

The answer to your question centers in part on the meaning of the word "critical." In the ordinary usage of the word this means to be fault-finding or censorious. There are, of course, other meanings of the word. However, in the study of the Bible the word means to evaluate, analyze, and also to study the historic, cultural, and linguistic backgrounds of the times during which the Bible was written. Such a critical study of the Bible has produced a tremendous volume of information, has clarified the meaning of many passages, and has made it possible for us to understand far more clearly the messages God would give to us. On the other hand there is a form of Biblical criticism which starts with certain preconceived ideas and which seeks to interpret the Bible in the light of these presuppositions. For instance, if one rejects the miraculous and the supernatural, one will reject these elements of the whole written Revelation from God. One can approach the Bible with a cold rationalistic attitude or one can do so with reverence and the desire to hear God speak. I have a friend, a physician, who says there is a difference between the attitude of a scientist dissecting a dead body in a dissecting hall and that of the surgeon who operates on a living person in the operating room. The Bible should be approached with the assurance that here we have God-breathed literature and that it is our privilege and joy to find out what He has to say. Try studying the Bible with that attitude and you will find out for yourself.

If the Bible is the Word of God, as you constantly say, why are there so many off-color stories in it?

Because there are so many sinners in the world. The Bible is not an idealistic fairy story. Rather it is a record of God's dealing with mankind and of many individual men and women. There is nothing which indicates the inspiration of the Scripture more than the factual and faithful record of men and their failures. For instance, one of the greatest men in the Bible is King David. And yet, the Bible tells us he was guilty of both adultery and murder. But it also tells us of his repentance and turning back to God. All of these records are for our warning and instruction. They show us how sinful man needs God and His redemptive work in Christ and they tell us of many who accepted this love and were transformed. There is one thing about the stories in the Bible where sinful acts are mentioned: they do not glorify sin, nor do they make people want to go out and copy them. The Bible always shows sin up for what it really is, an offense against God and something to be repented of and turned from.

Why do people who lie and cheat and hurt others always seem to win? What sense is there in trying to live a good life, and have hope and faith, when everything seems to go wrong when you do?

I'm afraid you have a wrong conception of what it means to "win." People who lie, cheat, and hurt others never win. They may gain a few dollars, they may gain a little niche in a certain stratum of society, but they never really win. They lose that most treasured of human possessions, a good conscience, they lose their reputations, and, in the end, if they don't repent they lose their souls.

It seems to me that you could lift your own sights a little bit. You say you try to live a good life, have hope and faith, and everything goes wrong. Goodness, hope, and faith carry a reward not preceded by a dollar sign. Christ didn't promise that if we would be good and follow Him, that we would share the rewards of the wicked. He spoke of "laying up treasures in heaven." Don't be good for reasons of earthly reward. Don't say "Lord, I'll have faith, if You will give me the rewards of financial success and security." Rather say "Lord, I'll serve You at all costs, win or lose in this life, I want to live for eternity." Then, you will be a winner and can say with Paul, "We are more than overcomers through Him that loved us and gave Himself for us." Christ said we must lose our life in order to find it.

I am a married man, with a good wife, and seven healthy, happy children. I work hard, and can barely make ends meet. But my neighbors who have no children get a new car every year, are able to go on trips, and eat much better than we do. I must confess I am a little envious of them. How can I keep from envying them?

I wouldn't be surprised to find out that your neighbors envy you more than you envy them. By almost every measure, *you are a rich man*. Happily married, a good wife, seven happy, healthy children and able to work. You are one of the wealthiest persons in town.

The Bible says: "Better is a dinner of herbs where love is, than a stalled ox and hatred therewith." If you could stand back and look at yourself objectively, you would see that you have every reason to be happy.

Perhaps you lack just one thing. The Bible says: "Better is a little with the fear [reverence] of the Lord than great treasure and trouble therewith." Your display of envy shows that you have a spiritual need. Slip to your knees tonight, and say: "Dear God, forgive me for being envious of my neighbor who in reality has much less than I. Help me to reverence Thee and to live for Thee." See if this doesn't help you.

In college I have been studying a course in ethics. I find that quite often a higher standard of ethics is held by secular thinkers than I experience in my contact with religious people. Is there any explanation for this?

Yes, there is an explanation for this. You must understand that culture and training have a great influence upon conduct. In the study of ethics, you are dealing with the highest ideal of human conduct that man is capable of expressing. Such expressions of conduct are theoretical, and the Bible clearly tells us that "When the gentiles that have not the law do by nature the things of the law, these, not having the law are a law unto themselves; in that they show the work of the law written in their hearts" (Romans 2:14–15). Most people know in theory what is right. What secular ethics does not and cannot provide is the motivation for right action. There is a great difference between the theory a man holds of conduct and the conduct itself.

Second, you must remember that the Christian is subjected to many temptations that are not common to those who are not Christians. On the average, you will find that the ethical and moral level of true Christians is now and always has been the highest. Only Christianity provides both the ethical standards and the adequate motivation.

I am a student of sociology and the Bible. I have come to the conclusion that the greatest curse on mankind is sex. If we had no sex it would solve most of the problems of mankind. Why did God give to the human race such a curse?

Sex was never given to be a curse, but a blessing. Fundamentally, sex expresses itself through the body. It is embedded in the physical body and is but one of the many functions of the body. Properly controlled and used, it ministers to our physical well-being, happiness, and usefulness. The sexual organs can be a constructive force—they can also be a destructive force. Sex is one of the most powerful factors in life. The sexual instinct, next to self-preservation, is the strongest instinct of mankind. There is no doubt that it has been misused. It has also caused wars and other types of social violence. However, God has regulated this force by laws written in the Bible and in the body itself. It is God ordained for the propagation of the human race. The sexual endowment of mankind, when properly expressed, is constructive in the highest degree. However, when these laws are violated and vice is practiced rather than virtue, there is a penalty. The penalty is very severe because the Creator endowed man with the powers of reproduction. Sex is the medium God uses in the propagation of human life. When nature is outraged, the results are weakness, mental dullness, insanity, and vile diseases. Sex can become a great servant but a terrible master. The Scripture teaches that we are to yield our bodies completely to God and let Him control our every thought. There is no sin in all the Bible condemned more than the sin of adultery and fornication.

What does the Bible mean when Jesus says in Luke 14:26: "If any man cometh unto me, and hateth not his own father and mother and wife and children and brethren and sisters, yea and his own life also, he cannot be my disciple"? This frightens me because I love my parents dearly.

Human language is always impoverished when we attempt to define and describe our relationships to Christ. This is one instance. The demand is not that we hate people, but rather that our love for Christ be so much higher and deeper and broader than the love we have for our dearest ones on earth that we would in any situation make all others second to Him. It is a word defining contrast. Our love for Him should be so unqualified that any other love, by contrast, would almost seem like hatred. You will notice that Jesus even included denial of self. People usually are lovers of themselves above other persons, but there is something so wonderful and so exclusive about our love for Christ that self must be denied. Jesus also said: "If any man will come after me, let him deny himself, and take up his cross and follow me." The Bible exhorts, love your parents and friends, but let your love for Christ be so far beyond human loves that they may by contrast appear to be far less than your love for Him.

I have been a Christian for several years. Although I still love Jesus and feel sure that I am His child, I know I am not making any definite progress. I seem always to be treading water or marking time. Is there any simple answer to this problem that you can give?

No complete answer to so complicated a problem can be given, but I can offer some specific suggestions.

1. Make sure you have been born again. Don't leave any doubts about this. Of course no one can grow who is not spiritually alive.

2. Never forget that the real source of all spiritual growth and progress is the Bible. Unless you systematically study the Bible, you cannot hope to make any true progress.

3. Prayer is important. It is a vital part of your life with God. Prayer is your true desire, expressed or hidden. If you desire what is promised in the Bible, then there is communication with God.

4. Obedience is the key to Bible knowledge. You don't read the Bible to satisfy curiosity but to find the practical answer to a real problem, and when you find the answer, you act decisively upon it.

5. Praise is essential. For every known blessing, give praise to God both privately and, when fitting, publicly. Praise is the action that puts you before others as an example. Do not avoid this public display of your love for God. Follow these steps, and you will experience the change at once.

It seems evident that America is forced into a secondary place as a world power, and that we are being threatened by Russia. If God is as you say, why would He allow such a godless nation to get into a position of world dominance? We have been upholding the principles of Godliness and decency, and yet we are losing ground.

The people of God have many times asked the same question. More than once it has happened that a very wicked nation overran a nation that was more righteous. One of the prophets complained about it saying: "Therefore the law is slacked and justice doth never go forth; for the wicked doth compass about the righteous."

It is essential for us to recognize the hidden purposes of God. A hymn frequently sung reads: "God moves in a mysterious way, His wonders to perform." In this matter we must walk by faith, for while we are in the midst of our dilemma, we are incapable of clear thinking. God's answer was: "I am working a work in your days which ye will not believe even if it were told you." Always remember that the outcome is safe in God's hand, and that however dark the day may be, there is every reason for hope for those who have committed their lives to God. Today may be our day of discipline and instruction.

Secondly, the sins of America are also great! We have sinned against a great light. Christ said: "To whom much is given much is required."

How can I believe God loves me when He destroyed our entire peach crop?

The Bible says: "Whom the Lord loveth He chasteneth." If life were all easy wouldn't we become flabby? When a ship's carpenter needed timber to make a mast for a sailing vessel he did not cut it in the valley, but up on the mountainside where the trees had been buffeted by the winds. These trees, he knew, were the strongest of all. Hardship is not our choice, but if we face it bravely it can toughen the fiber of our souls.

Even if you can't understand why your peach crop was destroyed you can still trust God. From disaster He can bring victory. A hurricane sweeps over a hillside, snapping the pines like matchsticks; but God has planted spruce seeds there, and in the sunlight they push up, making a new forest. Fire destroys a community. Then men and women arise to meet the challenge, building a more beautiful city. History has proved that God can build upon the ruins. But He needs the hands of consecrated men and women. Christ did not promise His followers ease or comfort. He said again and again: "Take up the cross and follow Me."

This experience could be your steppingstone to finding

Christ as your Lord and Saviour. That could be why it happened. When I was in Korea during the war, a young lad who had lost both eyes said to me: "I'm glad I came to Korea, because losing my eyesight brought me to Christ!" He had found Christ better than eyesight!

I have so often wondered if all the different denominations are pleasing to God. When Jesus left this world didn't He command that His apostles carry on His work? In Chapter 17 of John He prayed that the disciples might be one. Has this prayer of Jesus been in vain?

A book could be written on your question, but I will try to clarify the matter in a few words. It is not surprising that there are so many different branches of the Christian church. Even in the first century, the church became divided over trivial differences. Paul and Barnabas were loyal friends and faithful co-laborers in Christ. But they had a dispute because Barnabas insisted on taking Mark with them. The Bible says: "The contention was so sharp, that they departed asunder one from the other." This has been going on throughout the centuries. Perhaps it is God's way of keeping the stream of Christianity from becoming polluted and stagnated. Some time ago, one of the more perceptive leaders of Latin America said to me: "I have been reading that there is a movement on foot in America to bring all Protestant churches into one great church." He went on to say: "I think there is something wholesome in people worshiping God according to the dictates of their own conscience. I hope the time will never come when everyone will be 'rubber-stamped' into one ecclesiastical body."

We must remember that there is a difference between unity and union. I have found a great unity and spirit of Christian co-operation among the churches of the world. They believe, essentially, the same. Though they are not united in name, most of them are unified in spirit. We have seen as many as fifty different denominations working side by side for the glory of God. No, I don't think Christ's prayer for unity was prayed in vain.

What good is religion? There is a man in our neighborhood who never goes to church, runs around, and is mean to his family. But he has a bigger house, more money and has more reasons to be happy than people who are trying to live right.

You have told me quite a bit about your neighbor, and you have also told me quite a lot about yourself. Your question begins with: "What good is religion?" You then proceed to speak of the big house and the money your neighbor has. This reveals that you have a tinge of envy and that you are covetous of your neighbor's prosperity. My opinion is that both you and your neighbor need a better understanding of what faith in Christ, or, religion, as you say, really is.

You say that he has more reasons to be happy, but you infer that he is unhappy. You have almost answered your own question. You say that he is mean to his family and that he is unfaithful to his marriage vows, and yet you think he is a success. I would say that he is a miserable failure, and that if you envy such success, your life is doomed to failure too.

What good is religion? Well, true religion gives meaning and purpose to life. It crowns the home with love and affection. It brings a person into harmony with God's law, cures him of infidelity, and of selfish greed. We need to learn again the words of Jesus: "The abundance of a man's life consisteth not in the things which he possesseth" (Luke 12:15).

I wonder if you think religion can solve all of a person's problems? What becomes of psychiatric counseling and other kinds of therapy?

Religion can actually solve very few problems. In fact, religion frequently creates problems of both a social and personal nature. There is a great deal of confused thinking here, and often a religious attitude and way is equated with a personal faith in Jesus. Christianity is a personal relationship, and any religious forms that result are incidental more than vital. In marriage, the ceremony that publicly pronounces two people man and wife is incidental. The experiences that preceded and that follow are never formal and rehearsed but are spontaneous and vital. Unless a person lives in a conscious and vital relationship to Christ, the religious forms are empty. Jesus Christ can solve your problems when religion cannot. There is a place for psychiatric counseling when the problem is not one of spiritual significance. The good psychiatrist should know when the problem is spiritual and recommend the patient to a competent spiritual guide.

Do you think that the Gospel of the first century is relevant for our present time?

I might reply by asking you the same thing but stating it negatively. Do you think that the Gospel of the first century is not relevant for our present time? Has human personality changed significantly? Has human nature evidenced improvement recently? Are men and women gradually overcoming immorality, dishonesty, greed, passion, love of pleasure, hatred, and all the other evils named in the Bible? Certainly the Gospel of the first century is relevant, and more than relevant, it is the only answer to man's present moral and spiritual dilemma. As long as attempts are made to answer the deep spiritual problems by humanistic methods, we can only plan on failure. Not until the faith which was once and for all delivered unto the saints is preached in its fulness will we approach a remedy for our twentieth-century dilemma.

If one is a Christian and God directs and allows everything that happens to you, what takes place between God and you when you sin?

I believe the best answer to your question has to be answered by reference to an illustration. I ask you this question: What happens to the father-son relationship in everyday life when the son does something that is displeasing to the father?

The Bible does not tell us that we are going to live free from sin as long as we are in this body. The Bible says: "If we say that we have no sin, we deceive ourselves, and the truth is not in us" (I John 1:8).

Actually what will happen is that there is a rupture that takes place in our fellowship, and this fellowship is not completely restored until confession of that sin is made. In other words, we may still be sons of God without enjoying the fellowship that sons rightfully should have. There are thousands of Christians who do not have the joy and peace that fellowship with God brings. There is no joy or ecstasy quite like that of daily fellowship with God. Try it!

I simply cannot believe that Jesus was God. I believe He was a very good man and I try to live like Him.

If you are unwilling to believe that Jesus Christ is the Son of God you are in a very dangerous position, for faith in the deity of Christ is the very heart of the way of salvation. Only God could redeem us from our sins, and it is to God that we must look for salvation. In saying that you try to live like Christ you obviously do not know what you are saying. Can you live the sinless life that Christ lived? It is our sins which have separated between us and God, and it was to cleanse and forgive these sins that Christ came into the world. In forming an opinion about Christ, let me urge you to read the Bible and there see what God tells us about Him. Take the Gospel of John, for instance, and read and reread it and you will see how God sent His Son into the world to solve man's dilemma—a dilemma which is the result of sin in our hearts. When we try to be good, we never rise higher than ourselves. The Bible tells us that the very best a man can do is as filthy rags in God's sight. God is holy and pure and our only chance of coming into His presence is to become holy and pure, and we become just that when we accept Christ as our Saviour. His righteousness is given us, like a robe, so that God then sees the righteousness of Christ when He looks. Read John 3:16 again and again and ask God to make its meaning clear to your heart.

Don't you believe that emotional religion is a great danger? I recently met a religious person who is easily aroused emotionally whenever there is any discussion of God and Christ.

Emotion in religion is as dangerous as emotion in love. If it is dangerous to express religious relationships with emotion, then it is equally a dangerous thing to be emotional about a relationship such as that between a man and a woman. But who would wish to eliminate the emotional aspects of a courtship and marriage. They are among the highest and noblest feelings of human nature. They are an evil only when they are out of control and are not based upon a solid foundation of knowledge and understanding. Proper emotions are the result of a true love just as they are the result of a genuine faith in God. Love for God is never of the sensual type, but it is still love. Love is man's highest and most noble emotion. Always differentiate between legitimate emotions and mere emotionalism.

Chapter 24

Your Church and Its Problems

Why do you find such differences of opinion and such strong feelings on the part of some Christians about some matters of faith and church procedures?

There are several reasons. The Christian faith is so great in its implications that it is difficult for man to see it all. It is something like a diamond with many facets and we see only a part of the diamond at one time. Another reason is that there are times when we magnify some particular point beyond its rightful significance. There are things about the Christian faith which are essential, there are others which are important in varying degrees but which have no bearing on one's personal salvation. There may be times when men magnify a minor point and make it a major one. Then too the frailty and perversities of human nature may cause us to interpret certain truths from a purely human viewpoint, thereby losing their spiritual significance. While your question is interesting, let me suggest that you will be wise to look, not at the differences in the church but at the things on which historic Christianity has always agreed: the deity of our Lord, His death for our sins, His resurrection and His coming again among them. If we agree on the things about which the Bible is very clear, we can agree to disagree on many minor points. Let me further suggest that an argumentative spirit rarely honors the Lord.

Why do you always say that a new Christian should immediately unite with a church?

Why should a newborn baby have a home? It is as simple as that. A child can be born outside the home, and a person can become a Christian outside the church, but nurture and care are essential to the development of both. These can best be provided in the home in the case of the child, and in the church in the case of a Christian.

Every church is potentially a resurrection center. Into it come people who have been primarily concerned with their selfish affairs. In the church they broaden and come to feel the needs of other people. One of the signs of Christian life is the desire to share.

It is in the church that you are transformed from a self-centered individual into a self-sacrificing member of society.

Only the church provides the nurture for spiritual growth. Here we are taught to grow in the Word, and here we have the help of other Christians when we are tempted to stumble. The church is a storehouse of spiritual food whereby the inner man is fed, nourished, and developed into maturity. If it fails, it is not fulfilling its purpose as a church.

Not having been a Christian for long, I wonder if you can tell me how to choose a church? I don't want to get into one that does not preach the Gospel faithfully.

As an evangelist who works with all denominations, it is not my duty to tell people which church to join. However, there are certain desirable characteristics which may be found in churches of all denominations.

First, as you say, I would select a church which preaches the Gospel faithfully. However, it is not enough to be sound theologically. I would therefore choose a church which endeavored to practice what it preached, and to translate its beliefs into everyday life. I would choose a church where there was a degree of tolerance toward other Christians, for too often our Christian testimony is weakened by a raspy, critical spirit toward other Christians not of our group. I would choose a church that opened its arms to everyone with a spiritual need, regardless of their social standing, and that had a concern for the social sins of the community. I would choose a church which has a missionary vision and spirit, one which was willing to co-operate in every worthwhile effort to bring Christ to the world. And last, I would choose a church that was worthy of my tithes and offerings, and where I could find opportunity to give unstintingly of my talents and capabilities for the glory of God. And when I found that church, I would just hope that they would be lenient enough to accept me into their fellowship.

Some time ago I made a pledge to the church for missions. I made it large, mainly to impress people, and now I can't pay it. What are the legal problems involved? Can I be made to pay or what should be my course of action?

You remind me of the Pharisees that Jesus so roundly condemned in His times. They always wanted to be seen of men in the things they did. If they prayed, it was publicly, and if they gave alms, they wanted a trumpet to be blown to call attention to their munificence (Matthew 6:1–5). To such people Jesus said: "They have their reward." You had your reward at the time you made the generous pledge.

Legally, you can be sued, but I doubt if any church would do so. I am quite confident that no church group, however spiritually dead, would attempt to force collection of such a promise. But you still must answer to God. Actually your promise was supposedly made to Him. What do you intend to do about it? I see only one course of action now. Either you must make a public statement of your false intentions when you made the pledge or beg for time to honor it. If you did this, you would have a clear conscience toward men, if not toward God. As for the sinful aspect of it, you must repentantly turn to God, asking forgiveness in Jesus' name, and He who forgives every sin will also forgive you.

My friends claim I am not a Christian because I do not attend church. Can one be just as religious and good if he is not a member of a church?

I suppose it could be said that going to church will not make one a Christian. But of this we are even more sure: refusing to fellowship with believers will not make you one either.

I suppose you could live up to the principles of the Masonic Lodge without joining it. You could subscribe to the principles of the Rotary Club without being a Rotarian. But it seems to me that if you sincerely wanted to be a good Rotarian, or good Christian, you would do well to fellowship with those who have kindred goals and motives.

The church is the family of believers. Christ died, not only for the individual, but for the church. The Bible says: "He loved the church, and gave Himself for it." If Christ loved the church enough to die for it, we should love it enough to associate ourselves with it.

By joining a good spiritual church, we are letting the world know where our loyalties are. Even you admit that "your friends say you are not a Christian because you do not belong to church." If we really believe in Christ, the least we can do is to identify ourselves with others who believe. In this way your faith is strengthened, and your witness is buttressed.

Our church has such a demanding program, with many extra meetings; in fact there is something going on every night during the week. I realize this is important, but to attend all these services I would have to neglect my family. Can you help me with this problem?

Thank God that you are a member of a church that is doing something. However, I think your minister would be the first to agree that you should not neglect your family. A mother's chief responsibility is to her home and family, but that is not to say that she has no duty to her church.

The goal of a busy mother should be for balance. The Bible says there is a "time to weep, and a time to laugh, a time to rend, and a time to sew, a time for love, and a time for peace." If you plan your week, you will find ample time for your family, and also time for your church work. They make a happy and satisfying combination.

However, don't make too great a distinction between your home and the church, for their ultimate purpose is the same: the building of character in the lives of your children. Let your home be your congregation, and you its shepherd. Whether at church or at home you are making impacts that are eternal.

Our church is so well organized that there seems to be no place for the freshness of spontaneity, or individual expression. Sometimes I feel that I can't see Christ for the trimmings. Am I wrong in feeling this way?

No, I don't feel that you are wrong. I think perhaps you have a point here. I'm sure your pastor would welcome any constructive suggestions you may have along this line.

Most ministers regret that their membership does not participate more actively in the life of the church, and I am sure your minister would be glad for any sanctified "spontaneity" you may bring to the life of the church.

I hope the day will never come when the church abandons the "class meeting" and the prayer service. In these services everyone who so desires should have an opportunity for expression. The old-fashioned "testimony" meeting should be revived, for through this medium we can share our faith, and our triumphs, as well as our needs and mistakes with others.

But this is important: though opportunities for expression may be limited within the church walls, there is plenty of opportunity to witness to your neighbors and friends to the saving power of Christ. In fact, it is much more effective to witness to those who need Christ, rather than to those who already know Him. More power to you! Be spontaneous and expressive in your Christian witness.

Our church is planning a building program that I think is beyond our financial ability. My friends are enthusiastic.

Should I stand in opposition and still work in the church or should I leave as a matter of conscience?

As Christians we do not always find ourselves in total agreement in matters of policy. As long as there is no denial of the essentials of our faith, and as long as your friends do not cease to be your friends simply because you disagree, I would continue to work with them. There is no moral deviation here, but a matter of business judgment. We need to be able to disagree in love and still work together to bring men to Jesus Christ. State your objections and then when and if you are outvoted, accept it graciously and continue to work with them as friends and as brothers and sisters in Christ. Time may indicate that you were wrong and not they. If so, you still have your friends and your church.

I was raised in a family with very strong church ties. Now I am married and living in a community where there are no congenial churches. Do you think that my husband and I should try to start a new church?

Most of the major denominations have basically the same Christian doctrines. It is true that some are much closer to their original beliefs than others and for that reason congregations and ministers differ greatly. I would suggest that you make a study of the basic beliefs of the churches in your community and then join the one you feel most closely resembles your ideal. Remember that there is no perfect church and no perfect congregation. It can well be that God is opening up for you a new opportunity to serve Him through a church which needs your witness and help. Remember, also, that we sometimes confuse our prejudices with our beliefs. In any case you should join a church where you find spiritual help and strength each week and where you can join in the program of the church in reaching out to the unchurched in your community. It is impossible for me to answer your question in more than broad generalities because there are many details I know nothing of and also because this is a personal problem and God alone can lead you to a final decision which is right. You and your husband make this a matter of prayer and be sure that you follow God's leading in the matter. If you do that you will make no mistake.

When my husband and I were married, we both were Christians and went to church each Sunday. We now live in a suburb where our neighbors spend the weekends in sports and trips and we have been doing the same thing. We are miserable.

You should thank God that you are miserable. He is speaking to you through your conscience. Down deep in your heart, you know you have exchanged solid things which last for tinsel and temporary pleasure. Trips and sports have their rightful place in our lives, but when they take the place of church attendance and spiritual things in general, they are a snare and bring only disillusionment and sorrow. I know so many people who are in your predicament. I know others who were living as you are but who came to realize that life is more than recreation and a good time and who have started putting first things first in their lives. Today they are radiant with the joy Christ brings to hearts surrendered to Him. I have the idea that a lot of the couples around you are just as miserable as you are. They may not know the cause, but God is giving you an opportunity not only to correct the mistake you have made but also to lead them to see that life is far more than any of them now know. If you put Christ first in your personal lives, in your home, with your children and in the center of your church life, you will find that joy will supplant unhappiness and that the meaning of this life, and the one to come, becomes clear and bright. It will take moral courage to make the break and take the right step, but you will never regret it.

Do you think that if I begin to tithe it would help me solve my financial problem? I notice many preachers advocate tithing.

Tithing is certainly taught in the Old Testament and Jesus fully approved it as a practice. When the Pharisees boasted of it, He said: "This ought ye to have done and not left the other undone." Unfortunately, tithing has been frequently advocated as a mere device for money raising, and that is not its primary purpose. It is an act of worship and an expression of our faith in God. It is the most practical means of giving evidence to our claim that all we have is the Lord's.

But tithing will not solve your financial problem. If I understand your question, you are really trying to bribe God rather than worship Him. You cannot purchase the favor of God with money, because He is not in need of the little you have. By your giving, God gives you the opportunity of sharing in the work of spreading the Gospel and being a co-worker with Him.

We are members of a new and struggling church. Our young pastor is making demands for financial support. Do you think it is wrong for him to make such demands, and is there any reason why he can't do other work?

I do not know your young minister, but I would say that if he is a deeply spiritual man, with a desire to give more time to his calling, you have a duty to do your best for him financially. The Bible teaches: "The laborer is worthy of his hire." The Bible also teaches, in Galatians 6:6: "Let him that is taught in the Word communicate unto him that teacheth in all good things."

One of the most underpaid groups of men in the world are ministers. Almost every survey indicates that the average minister's pay is far below what it should be.

On the other hand, I have never felt that any minister should make a demand. Perhaps you have used the wrong word in describing a legitimate suggestion or proposition from his point of view.

To answer your question more specifically, there is nothing fundamentally wrong with a minister working. Paul did in his time, and many others have done so in the long history of the church. That does not mean that it is the best way to do it. Your pastor cannot give the time nor the effort to his ministry if he must earn a living by other means. You would probably be the first to criticize if he failed to visit the sick or preach a good sermon on Sunday. I suggest the people give a little extra.

We hear so much said about churches giving dinners and such for the purpose of making money for the church. Do you think it is right for churches to have dinners?

I think the church fellowship dinners are a fine thing. Jesus ate with His disciples in the Upper Room, and I believe there is something edifying about God's people eating and fellowshiping together.

In regard to the church competing with the restaurants for the purpose of raising money, that is another question. Personally, I believe that if Christians paid their tithe, and gave of their substance as liberally as they ought, there would be no need of church suppers for profit. I have noticed that tithing churches have more time to spend winning the lost in their community than religious groups which must resort to secular means of raising their finances. There is not only a great spiritual blessing in tithing, but it releases valuable time for Christians to do more important things for Christ. A classic appraisal of this problem came from Jesus' words to Martha when she complained that Mary was shirking her culinary duties. He said: "Mary hath chosen the better part." It is not that "serving tables" is so wrong, it is simply that Christians can employ their time a lot more gainfully.

Our church is always asking for money for missions and other causes. We get the impression that they are more interested in money than in the needs of our own community. Should the church overstress money?

It might interest you to know that mission giving, per capita, amounts to only one cent for the church people of America. As Christians, I hardly think we are overdoing the matter of foreign missions. We need a hundred thousand missionaries in the spiritual and technical fields. Dr. Frank Laubauch, an authority in this field, says that "We have but one short year to fight Communism." He says that if we don't awaken to our responsibility in helping starving, backward people to help themselves that we shall be six hundred million facing two billions of the enemy and we cannot possibly survive.

Of course, missionary work is more than economical in its impact. Millions who have never heard the name of Jesus deserve to own the joy and peace that come in knowing Him and His power to forgive sins.

If your church is overemphasizing finances, it is probably because its constituents have failed to give God His share. I have never heard a person who is giving God what belongs to Him complain about the demands for money. It is usually the fellow who is in debt to God who gripes when the preacher mentions money.

We have recently moved into a new community where there is no church of our denomination. There is a church here with which we can agree with few reservations. Should we drive a great distance to a church of our own denomination, or could we serve where we are? They have asked me to teach a Sunday school class.

I believe in denominational loyalty, but I also believe that Christians should witness where they live. Unless we show an interest and love for those in our community, people might get the idea that you are religious snobs—which of course you are not.

You say that you agree with the doctrine of the local church with few reservations. I have found that nonessentials separate people more often than essentials. In reading the history of denominations, it is interesting to note that the great divisions have always resulted from somewhat minor differences. More important is to maintain a Christian attitude in spite of the differences between us. Some people call that "compromise"—others see it as Christian charity.

I have made up my mind to fellowship with all those who love Jesus Christ with all their heart, and are seeking to win men to Him. At the moment I am being criticized by a few people for doing this, but I would rather lose a few friends than the blessing and favor of my Lord. If you feel that you can be a blessing to these people who don't see quite eye to eye with you on every point, by all means serve where you will be the greatest blessing.

Chapter 25

The Firmest Foundation

How can we know what is right and what is wrong? There are so many conflicting ideas, and one becomes confused. Is there really any rule to go by?

The Bible says: "If any man will do his will, he shall know of the teaching, whether it be of God." I think before one can know what is right and wrong, he must first align himself with God. Only then is he in a position to do right.

J. Wilbur Chapman once said: "The rule that governs my life is this: Anything that dims my vision of Christ, or takes away my taste for Bible study, or cramps my prayer life, or makes Christian work difficult, is wrong for me, and I must, as a Christian, turn away from it."

When I have a problem of deciding right from wrong I always give it three tests. First, I give it the common-sense test, and ask if it is reasonable. Then, I give it the prayer test. I ask God if it is good and edifying. Then, I give it the Scripture test. I see if the Bible has anything to say for or against it. Then, I may add a fourth: the conscience test. But the most important thing is to follow Jesus' suggestion: "If any man wills to *do His will* he shall know."

What Christian grace in my heart can make me a better Christian and a better witness for Christ?

The greatest Christian grace is love; not the sentimental feeling often called love today but that deep regard for the welfare of others which will prompt us to help them when they need help; to be sympathetic when sympathy is needed; to make us say kind things about people instead of being critical; to make us long to win them to Christ if they are not Christians. Love is at the very heart of everything which comes from God, for He is love. It was love which prompted the sending of His Son into the world to die for our sins. It is love which is mentioned first when the Apostle Paul enumerates the fruits of the Spirit. It is love which must characterize our attitude to God and man, if we are to fulfill His law. In Matthew 22:37–38 we read: "Thou shalt love the Lord thy God with all thy heart, and with all thy soul, and with all thy mind. This is the first and great commandment." Following this, Christ said: "The second is like unto it, Thou shalt love thy neighbor as thyself." After that, Christ tells us: "On these two commandments hang all the law and the prophets." It is God's love which should constrain us. The Bible says: "Herein is love, not that we love God, but that He loved us, and sent His Son to be the propitiation of our sins." If you have a loving heart, you will bear fruitful witness for Christ.

I have recently begun to read the New Testament. Now I am told that the church existed before the New Testament, and therefore is in possession of more authority than the Bible itself. Can you explain the problem to me so that I can study with restored confidence?

Historically, the church was in existence before the New Testament. That does not place it in authority above it, for you will notice that the writers always appeal to the existing Old Testament as authority. Also, you will notice that God approved the genuineness of the work and the dependability of the writer, by miraculous demonstration and by general consent of the body of believers in every place. The books we call canonical were able by the weight of their contents to separate themselves from all spurious and pseudo books. The evidence is in the books themselves, not alone because of their historical accuracy and approval, but on the basis of the power of their combined message, and the vitality they exhibit in every generation causes this work to commend itself to you as being superior to continuing organizations or conflicting voices in any age. Its power to transform lives is its best apologetic.

I find it helpful to read my Bible in the train on my way to work each morning. Some of my friends tell me I ought not to do this, as it is flaunting my religion in the face of others and probably makes them feel uncomfortable. What do you advise?

If I were you I would not worry too much about what other people say or think in a matter of this kind. If you bother unduly about the opinions of others you will never do anything at all!

By all means read your Bible in the train if you find this helpful. While those around you are filling their minds with the bad news about man in their daily papers, steep yourself in the good news about God in His precious Word!

Of course, I will admit that a crowded railway car is not the best place for reading the Bible, for it is not easy to concentrate in such circumstances; and real Bible study requires concentration. Nevertheless, it is well to use every moment of the day to the best advantage, and there is no doubt that a great deal of time is wasted on journeys which could be employed in a much better way.

I do not quite understand why the fact of your reading the Bible in public should make others feel uncomfortable—unless they are non-Christians or backsliders. And in that case they have no right to be comfortable! They need to be aroused out of their comfortable indifference and reminded of the claims of God's Word; and it may be that your example may serve to remind them of the Book they have neglected.

I would like to have a better understanding of the Christian religion, but never seem to get much out of the Bible when

I read it. Can you tell me of some book or commentary that will answer the question in a more simple way?

No book ever takes the place of the Bible. It is its own best commentary. I would urge you to go on studying the text of the Bible itself. Only when you find it in the Bible are you sure it is Scriptural truth. As a help, I would make a few simple suggestions.

First, be open-minded. If you begin with a prejudice, you will be blind, or else you will read into the Bible what is not really there.

Second, act upon the basis of what you discover. The Bible is a guidebook, leading men to God in a personal faith. Like a map or guidebook, it will show you the way, but you must take it one step at a time.

Third, ask God to enlighten your mind. In other words, read it prayerfully. The sound of the words will not help, for you must understand what you read. God provides enlightenment for those who wish it.

Finally, continue your study. Be patient, for the knowledge of God comes gradually and slowly. The fact that God is infinite makes the study of His word a lifetime occupation. The Bible is to your soul what bread is to your body. You need it daily. One good meal does not suffice for a lifetime.

In beginning to study the Bible for myself, are there any particular matters of method I should observe?

Very definitely there are. First, you must read it with a desire to know and to accept any truth you discover. You can be critical but you must be fair and open-minded. Second, you must read systematically, and not at random. The Bible will yield the richest blessing in the long run to those who study systematically. Begin regular reading of the Bible from beginning to end in your morning Bible reading time, and concentrate on a specific book in your evening time. I would suggest the Gospel of John and then the book of Romans. Third, you must study prayerfully, relying upon God to enlighten your mind and enable you to understand what you read. Pray frequently as you read and you will discover a fellowship with God that is both intimate and satisfying. Fourth, make use of dependable helps but do not rely upon them. Many helps are actually a hindrance. Make sure you are learning the Bible and not the views of some individual. You may be in perfect agreement but there is a blessing in knowing you got it from God.

I am a new Christian and I honestly want to know and do God's will but how can I know what His will for me really is?

There are many ways by which God leads us but it is only when we have minds and hearts surrendered to Him that we sometimes hear His voice. God speaks to us through the Holy Spirit, sometimes while we are praying. I know a man who was faced with a very difficult problem. He was an earnest Christian and he prayed about this particular problem and while he was praying he had a clear sense of the answer, so much so that he got up from his knees and wrote it down. Later in the day, during a conference in which the problem was under discussion, he read this statement. Immediately the entire group, although they had differed sharply one with the other, felt this was the answer and unanimously agreed. As a result, an issue which had divided Christians for months was resolved in absolute harmony. God sometimes leads men through the words or acts of other people. He often gives direct leading as we pray about it and read our Bibles. There are times when a group of individuals may come to a conclusion which indicates how one of them should act. The important thing is to be willing to do God's will. When that is true, God will surely make it known. Many Christians have experienced the fulfillment of the words of the Prophet Isaiah: "And thine ears shall hear a word behind thee, saying, This is the way, walk ye in it, when ye turn to the right hand, and when ye turn to the left" (30:21). Another promise is found in Proverbs 3:5–6: "Trust in the Lord with all thine heart; and lean not unto thine own understanding. In all thy ways acknowledge Him, and He shall direct thy paths."

For the benefit of those who are confused, would you explain your position on tithing? Should we give a tenth of our gross income or a tenth of what we have left after expenses are paid?

I can only tell you my personal convictions in the matter. If I were to wait until all expenses were paid before I tithed my income, there would be none left for the Lord. Income means what comes in, and if we give one tenth of our income to Kingdom work, then we must give a tithe of our gross income.

The trouble with too many of us is that we try to see how little we can get by with rather than how much we can do for God. Even the federal government recognizes tithing and charitable giving as a citizen's duty and allows such to be deducted from income tax. I have had many people tell that nine tenths of their income went farther with God's blessing on it than ten tenths of it did without His blessing. We have found that true in our own experience. Did not God say "Bring ye *all the tithes* into the storehouse . . . and prove me now herewith, saith the Lord of hosts, if I will not open ye the windows of heaven, and pour you out a blessing, that there shall not be room enough to receive it" (Malachi 3:10).

Chapter 26

How Should I Serve?

I am a fireman and have recently accepted Christ as my Saviour. Some of my fellow firemen make fun of me, but others have congratulated me for taking a stand for Christ. What should I say to those who laugh at the reality of religion?

For one thing, I think you should develop a little sense of humor. You might tell those fellows who take religion so lightly to keep their shovels handy, they might need them to stoke some fire in the world to come.

Seriously, I can sympathize with your problem. It is not an easy thing to take the jibes of fellows you like just because you have taken a stand for Christ. You want their good will, but not at the expense of denying your Lord. I have an idea that they are just testing you to see if you are really sincere in your faith in Christ. Stand up to them like a man, but avoid any bitterness or anger toward them.

Down deep in their hearts they admire you, and, like a fellow who gives a new car a test before he buys it, they may be in the market for faith in Christ also, but they just want to see if it works under pressure. This is where you can be a real witness. Sometimes the less said the better. Silence and patience are often the best rebuke to critics. Remember when Jesus was brought before His critics "He opened not His mouth." It sometimes takes more grace to keep your mouth shut than to open it. You will find as you patiently take these criticisms that your faith and strength will grow, and I dare say that some of your buddies will be following in your footsteps before too long.

You say that all Christians should witness for Christ. I am a Christian but, unfortunately, I am shy and not a gifted conversationalist. Does God expect me to be as good a witness as those who are blessed with the gift of speech?

There are many ways of witnessing, and I am not at all sure that vocal witnessing is always the most effective. What you are and the way you conduct yourself are much more important than what you say. Words are soon forgotten, but a Christian attitude will be long remembered by those who behold it.

Then, too, you can write letters which exalt Christ, and glorify Him. If you have a friend or relative who is not yet a Christian, write them a note in which you ask them to share the joy and peace you have found through Him.

Your devout, consecrated life in a hundred ways can be a solid witness for the Lord. However, I don't think you should rule out the possibility of putting in a word of spoken testimony either. You must talk at times about other things, although you say conversation doesn't come easy for you. You will find witnessing for Christ will come quite natural, if you practice it with the same regularity as you would for achieving any other worthwhile skill. It is quite possible that by becoming more articulate for God, that you may even overcome your shyness. "Let the redeemed of the Lord say so."

The Lord has done much for me, but many of my friends say I should not talk so much about the Lord. They say I should just live it, but not talk so much. Should I be silent about His blessings, or should I tell them?

The Bible gives the most direct answer to your question. You should do both! A good life without a word spoken fails to explain why it is good, and the spoken word without the good life is a mockery. Jesus said: "If ye confess Me before men, I will confess you before My Father Who is in heaven, but if ye deny Me before men, I will deny you before My Father Who is in heaven." The Bible also says: "If thou shalt confess with thy mouth the Lord Jesus and believe in thine heart that God hath raised Him from the dead, thou shalt be saved." The same Bible says: "But wilt thou know, O vain man, that faith without work is barren?" Yes, you should tell what the Lord has done, and you should also so live that all men will be able to see a demonstration of His transforming power in your life. This way they too can know what Christ can do for them.

I want to direct my friends to Christ, yet when I try to explain the virgin birth and such things to them they just say I'm believing things that no one believes any more, and they think that I am queer. Should I just be silent about it, because if I don't, I'll lose contact with them anyhow?

You are making the same mistake that many zealous persons make when trying to influence others for Christ. There are many truths that are a part of the Christian faith which no enlightened Christian will deny. But they are not the truths we stress when bringing the Gospel to the lost. It is a matter of what pertinent truth should be presented that the sinner can understand.

Everyone can understand history, and the Gospel story took place in history. The birth, the sinless life, the death of Christ by crucifixion, and His resurrection are all history. So is sin in the human heart a matter of both history and personal experience. The lost person must be confronted with his own sinful condition and then with the fact that Christ died and rose for him. These he accepts by faith. When once that person received the Saviour, he has a new vision and new insight. The matters he formerly rejected or could not understand, he now can grasp, for he has a new personality and new understanding.

For two years I have spent most of each Sunday afternoon working with some young people in a neighborhood Sunday school. It has been discouraging work and my wife is urging me to stop and spend that time with her and visiting friends. What do you advise?

If these young people are being taught the Bible and about Christ, our Saviour and Lord, you must not become discouraged. Although you may not have seen results so far you can rest assured that God has used and is using this work in some of these young hearts. All of us like to see results but God does not always work that way. I once heard a missionary tell of his early days in China. For seven years he did not win one convert to Christianity: then one came, then more and more. When he died a few years ago, there was a flourishing church in the city where he had labored for so long. This church had its own pastor and officers and was completely self-supporting and in no way dependent on the mission or missionaries. The Apostle Paul, in writing to the Corinthian Christians, knew some of them were discouraged and he wrote: "Therefore, my beloved brethren, be ye steadfast, unmovable, always abounding in the work of the Lord, forasmuch as ye know that your labour is not in vain in the Lord." Let me urge you to continue in your work in this Sunday school. Pray daily for these young people. Pray that the Holy Spirit will guide you in what you say and do. Ask your wife to join you in this work. I can assure you on the promise of God's word that some day you will be thankful that you remained faithful.

Since I gave my heart to Christ, I'm not happy working as an electrician. I feel I want to give all my life to Jesus. What do you think I should do?

Certainly you should surrender all your life to Christ. But don't make the mistake of thinking only preachers and missionaries do this. Jesus, Himself, was a carpenter. You can serve the Master wherever you are. Ask yourself: "What would Jesus do if He was in my place?"

Get down on your knees and ask God for guidance. Perhaps He'll tell you to give up your present work, and get the necessary training to be a full-time Christian minister. If you feel led to do this you must be prepared for a long, hard road ahead. After years of specialized training in one field it is difficult to start study in another. However, if this is the Lord's will for your life, He'll sustain you.

Don't make this decision hastily. Be sure you are listening to God's voice, and not your own. Our Heavenly Father may remind you that you can witness for Him right where you are. Support the church with your time as well as your money. Teach a Sunday school class, or set aside one evening each week to call on strangers in the community, or those who don't know the Saviour. Remember that honest work, well done, is always service for Christ. As you bring light into homes and shops you are working with God. By your friendliness and understanding you can bring Christ's presence to all you meet. If you give people love and sympathy they will open their hearts to you, and every day you'll find an opportunity to tell at least one person about the Lord Jesus Christ.

Immediately after graduating from college I went into the Army and am due to be discharged in a few months. I honestly want to serve God but I don't know what He wants me to do.

I am convinced that anyone who honestly wants to know God's will for his life will be led to a clear understanding of God's plan for him. This has its foundation in a personal faith in Jesus Christ as Saviour. Up in the White Mountains there is a stone profile of the "Old Man of the Mountain." Viewed from any perspective other than the profile it is but a mass of rock. Christ must be seen from the standpoint of His being the Son of God and from the fact that He died on the Cross for our sins. Otherwise the Cross is foolishness. In the Irish Channel there are a series of lights which the pilot of a ship must line up before entering one of the harbors. In determining God's will for our lives, once we have given our hearts to Christ, there are certain factors which converge in giving us spiritual leading. First there is the inward impulse coming from the leading of the Holy Spirit. Then there is the Bible which corroborates our sense of Divine guidance. Finally, God often uses a trend of circumstances through which He indicates His leading. In this connection Proverbs 3:5–6 is a wonderful promise. "Trust in the Lord with all thine heart; and lean not unto thine own understanding. In all thy ways acknowledge Him, and He shall direct thy paths." Here is a definite promise. Believe it and act on it. God will not fail you.

In your Oklahoma City meetings, I accepted Christ but as I am fifty years of age I am not sure how I can best serve Him. What do you advise?

Unless you are engaged in a business which is in itself unworthy of a Christian, the place to start serving the Lord is right where you work. There is no more effective witness for Christ than for people to see our lives completely changed and dedicated to Him. It is probable that you will be spared for many years of fruitful service to the Lord. You can pray daily that the words of the 90th Psalm may be your own: "So teach us to number our days, that we may apply our hearts unto wisdom." God has promised "As thy days, so shall thy strength be." This does not necessarily mean physical strength but the strength to know and do His holy will. In your new-found faith, ask God to give you the opportunities each day which He would have you have. Be faithful in reading your Bible and make it a part of your life. Make prayer something vital and practical. Let the joy of your salvation shine on your face. If you do these things, you will find opportunities for serving Christ opening up to you on every hand. Finally, speak to someone about your Saviour every day. It will make Him real and precious to you and you may win others to Him by your testimony.

I have for some time felt the urge to go to the mission field. I have been stirred through the preaching of some fine men of God. However, I have a wife who is very frail and a father who is elderly and dependent on me. I would have to go to some school for training and many other complications make it seem impossible. Am I disobeying God if I don't follow this impulse?

Any Christian is disobeying God who does not follow the impulse to be a missionary. In fact, every Christian has that commission, and not just a few. Your feeling about being a missionary is normal for the believer and you both can and must obey the call. The question is: Where will you go to evangelize? What makes you think you must travel some great distance? If God wanted you to go to some distant land, He would certainly provide a way. The fact that you have responsibilities and obstacles is without doubt God's way of showing you where you are to do your missionary work. The special training is for those who are to do a special work, but you can begin now in your own community to spread the knowledge of Christ to those who have not yet heard. Let God direct you a step at a time, and as you engage in the glorious work of missions at home, you can still be looking for the open door. If you have success at home, you can depend on it when you go elsewhere. Meanwhile, pray, plan, and work in keeping with your present desire and God will give you clear direction in His time.

When I was a young man, I felt God's call to preach the truth to my people. I refused to obey His call and later got married. Now I feel the call again, but with a wife and family I cannot get the training or leave my work. Am I sinning now that I cannot serve Him?

Always remember, first of all, that if you have come to God seeking forgiveness for your past sins and failures, they are forgiven and forgotten by Him, even though you may reproach yourself and never forget. The Bible says: "If we confess our sins, He is faithful and just to forgive us our sins, and to cleanse us from all unrighteousness" (I John 1:9). Do not reproach yourself now for a sin committed years ago if you have repented and sought forgiveness.

Remember, secondly, that if God is again calling you to

serve Him in any way, such as preaching in your case, He will provide the opportunity. God's call always includes an open door, but God's open door also may be accompanied with opposition. Make sure you are entirely willing to do His will, and then when you have done your best, you can leave it to Him to make a way. Most important, don't forget that you can serve Him right where you are and that may be His calling for you. The early church were nearly all laity. Most of our churches make too great a distinction between pastor and laity. We need dedicated laymen as much as we need full-time preachers.

I am a married woman and have two small children. I feel that God is calling me to do missionary work. Do you think I should leave my little family and apply for work with some missionary board? I am forty years of age.

My dear woman, the greatest missionary service a married woman can render is to be a devoted Christian mother. Let your home be your parish, your little brood your congregation, your living room a sanctuary, and your knee a sacred altar.

God has entrusted and dignified you with motherhood. There is no task or no calling higher than that. If, when you have discharged your responsibility to your family, you have extra time, there are people in your community who need Christ. And your church undoubtedly has many opportunities for Christian service. Yes, indeed become a missionary, but let it be under your own roof, and in your own neighborhood.

I am engaged in evangelistic preaching and work as a miner to help pay expenses. I seek to witness for the Lord at all times. I do need some recreation, and enjoy fishing very much. Is recreation of this kind the will of God, according to such Scriptures as Colossians 3:1 and I John 2:15?

God has made provision for rest and recreation for His creatures from the very beginning. Even Jesus called His disciples to come apart from the regular activity of the day to rest awhile. When we are told to "seek those things which are above," we are given the guiding principle of life. It would apply as much in work as in pleasure. When we are told that we are not to love the world, neither the things that are in the world, we are told not to have our aim fixed on making the perfect adjustment to a world order that will someday pass away. We are to have our relationship to God as the first matter to be cared for. Our supreme love is for Him and not for this world order.

God has entrusted you with the care of your physical body. As the temple in which He dwells, it deserves the best care you can give it. Wholesome recreation is necessary and beneficial. When it is controlled and used for His glory, it is as much a necessity as the food we eat and the clothes we wear.

We are a young couple with four children. We both have the feeling that my husband should enter the ministry and serve the Lord. What do you think about this? At what age does a man usually enter this field of service?

You say you both have the feeling your husband should "serve the Lord." Of course you can do this in a lay capacity, as well as in a ministerial capacity. We make a mistake in thinking that a minister is the only man of God. As Christians, we are all to be people of God, and striving to serve Him acceptably.

I would say two things to you both about entering the ministry. First, don't contemplate being a preacher, if you can be content doing anything else. My call to preach (and others have said they had a similar experience) was the result of a compelling urge to devote myself to the ministry, and a complete lack of interest in any other vocation. That was God's way of outlining my life's work. If the ministry appeals to you as a desirable profession, with allurements of social and financial compensations, by all means give up the idea. But if there is an inner urge to win men to Christ, and an unquenchable desire to preach the Gospel, by all means do it.

Second, no man is ever too old to give himself to full-time Christian service. If this is God's will for you, drop everything and begin your preparation. He will see you through, and as you obey Him, you will find it the greatest adventure imaginable, for you will be a working partner with God.

With all the hoodlumism and juvenile delinquency, I often wonder what the world of tomorrow will be like. One wonders if there are any good, wholesome young people any more. I have no children of my own, but I wonder what an ordinary person like myself can do to help solve this problem?

I well realize the prevalence of juvenile delinquency and the pitfalls of today's youth, but I would be the first to say that I have never lost faith in our young people. Though there are 3 per cent of our youth who are delinquent, that leaves 97 per cent who are not. If you could be in our crusades and see the hundreds of young people in the services, and many of them leading their friends to Christ, you would be encouraged. There are thousands and thousands of fine, consecrated young people in America who contemplate going into full-time Christian service. A sixteen-year-old wrote me recently, saying: "I don't think you realize the large number of youth today who have dedicated their lives to Christ and plan to go into Christian service. In my high school there are ten who have made their choice to that effect."

What can you do? Encourage the young people in your community to live for Christ. Invite them into your home. Fellowship with them, and show them that you are interested in them. The trouble is that young people are searching and many good people haven't helped them to find the right things.

Chapter 27

The End of the World

I recently heard a preacher say that the atom bomb was the instrument God had designed to destroy the earth. I can't remember the verse, but do you believe that such a thing is taught in the Bible?

Whether or not that is the means God has designed to destroy the earth is a matter of speculation. There are some things we are reasonably certain of according to the Bible. We do know that a day of judgment is coming and that the time is a matter of the utmost secrecy. "As a thief in the night" is the way Peter described it. Whenever that momentous day does come, we know that it will end with a dissolving of the now existing elements. The Bible says: "The heavens will pass away with a great noise and the elements shall be dissolved with fervent heat, and the earth and the works that are therein shall be burned up" (II Peter 3:10). It does appear that the same physical laws that bring about the release of energy in the atom will operate in the dissolution of the earth, but that does not mean that man will do it with an atomic bomb. Most important is that we should be prepared. We do not need to know surely how it will come about, but rather that we are in a state of readiness when it does.

Do you really believe that this world will come to an end?

Yes, I believe that this world, as we know it, will come to an end. When, I do not know, but all history is pointing forward to a climactic event when everything now seen will be purified by fire. This is not fanciful imagination but the clear and repeated testimony of the Bible. In both the Old and New Testaments we have this climax foretold. Our Lord Himself said such would take place. A study of this universe, in which this world is but an infinitesimal speck, shows that any one of a number of factors could bring about this physical cataclysm.

The Bible says: "But the day of the Lord will come as a thief in the night; in the which the heavens shall pass away with a great noise, and the elements shall melt with fervent heat, the earth also, and the works that are therein shall be burned up." This same Bible says: "Believe on the Lord Jesus Christ, and thou shalt be saved, and thy house."

Do you believe that Jesus Christ is going to make a visible, physical return to this earth?

Yes, I believe this with all my heart, not because of the opinions of others but based solely on what the Bible so plainly teaches. In the Old Testament there are prophecies which can only be fulfilled by our Lord's return. In the New Testament we find over three hundred references to the second coming. For instance, Christ Himself said again and again that He is coming back. For instance: "I go to prepare a place for you and if I go and prepare a place for you I will come again and receive you unto Myself." Again He said: "Hereafter shall ye see the Son of Man sitting on the right hand of power, and coming in the clouds of heaven." In I Thessalonians Paul says: "For the Lord Himself shall descend from heaven with a shout, and the voice of an archangel, and with the trump of God." His coming is going to be visible: "Behold He cometh with clouds; and every eye shall see Him." When our Lord ascended up into heaven, two men suddenly stood by the disciples and said: "Ye men of Galilee, why stand ye gazing up into heaven? This same Jesus, which is taken up from you into heaven, shall so come in like manner as ye have seen Him go into heaven." In the book of Revelation Christ says: "I am Alpha and Omega, the beginning and the ending, saith the Lord, which is, and which was, and which is to come, the Almighty." The fact that Christ is going to return is a glorious hope and also a stern warning. "Today is the day of salvation."

On what grounds do you base your statement that Jesus Christ is coming back? Did not Christ say, "Lo, I am with you always, even unto the end of the world"?

We look for the return of the Lord because He said many times that He would come and because it is one of the most frequently mentioned subjects in all the Bible. Christ is with us today through His Holy Spirit and He will be with Christians and with the church down to the end of the age. When He ascended up into heaven after His resurrection His disciples were standing looking upward when two men stood by them and said: "Ye men of Galilee, why stand ye gazing up into heaven? This same Jesus, which is taken up from you into heaven, shall so come in like manner as ye have seen him go into heaven." This climactic event of history is yet in the future. It will be sudden, climactic and final. It will take the unbelieving world by surprise and men will try to hide from His holy presence. It will be the occasion of the resurrection of believers and the sudden gathering together of believers to be with the Lord. There are many details about His return on which men can merely speculate. The important thing is that He is coming again and that we yet have time to trust in Him as our Saviour and Lord. When He comes all men must face Him, either as Saviour or Judge.

THE 500,000 COPY NATIONAL BEST SELLER
AT $3.95. BILLY GRAHAM CALLS IT THE MOST
IMPORTANT BOOK HE HAS EVER WRITTEN!

Billy Graham
WORLD AFLAME

75146/75¢

Other titles by Billy Graham:

PEACE WITH GOD.................................50054/50¢
THE SECRET OF HAPPINESS................50193/50¢

If your bookseller does not have these titles, you may
order them by sending retail price, plus 10¢ for mail-
ing and handling to: MAIL SERVICE DEPARTMENT,
POCKET BOOKS, A Division of Simon & Schuster,
Inc., 1 West 39th St., New York, N.Y. 10018. Not
responsible for orders containing cash. Please send
check or money order.

PUBLISHED BY
POCKET BOOKS